The Guide to GYMNASTICS FOR CHILDREN

Although every care has been taken in the preparation of this work, the author or the publisher cannot in any way be held responsible for the information (formulas, recipes, techniques, etc.) contained in the text. In the case of specific problems - often unique to each individual reader - it is recommended that a qualified person be consulted in order to obtain the most complete, accurate and up-to-date information possible. EDITORIAL DE VECCHI, S.A.U.

© Editorial De Vecchi, S. A. 2021
© [2021] Confidential Concepts International Ltd., Ireland
Subsidiary company of Confidential Concepts Inc, USA

ISBN: 978-1-64699-684-1

The current Criminal Code provides: "Anyone who, for profit and to the detriment of a third party, reproduces, plagiarizes, distributes or publicly communicates, in whole or in part, a literary, artistic or scientific work, or its transformation, interpretation or artistic performance fixed on any type of support or communicated by any means, without the authorization of the holders of the corresponding intellectual property rights or their assignees, shall be punished with imprisonment of six months to two years or a fine of six to twenty-four months. The same penalty shall be imposed on anyone who intentionally imports, exports or stores copies of such works or productions or performances without the said authorization". (Article 270)

Anna Salaris

The Guide to
GYMNASTICS FOR CHILDREN

INDEX

INTRODUCTION	7
GYMNASTICS AS A GAME	9
PSYCHOMOTOR DEVELOPMENT	
OF THE CHILD	11
Psychomotor Skills	12
Coordination	
Body Perception	12
Out-of-Body Perception	13
Physical Capacities	14
From One to Six Years	15
From Seven to Twelve Years	16
A FEW TIPS	
BEFORE YOU START	17
When to Do the Exercises	17
Where to Do the Exercises	18
Material Required	18
HOW TO DO THE EXERCISES	19
From One to Six Years	20
From Seven to Twelve Years	21
READY TO PLAY!	
FROM ONE TO SIX YEARS	25
Games With the Body	25
Exercise 1	26
Exercise 2	27
Exercise 3: The Elephant	28
Exercise 4: The Frog	29
Exercise 5: The Puppet	30
Exercise 6: The Tree	31
Exercise 7: The Flower Waking up	32
Exercise 8: The Flower that Goes to Sleep	33
Exercise 9: Nailing Nails	34
Exercise 10: The Indian and Cavalry	35
Exercise 11	36
Exercise 12	37
Exercise 13: The Traffic Light	38
Exercise 14: The Tightrope Walker	42
Exercise 15: The Tightrope Walker Rising and Falling	43
Exercise 16	44
Exercise 17: The Trunk Tree	45
Exercise 18	46
Exercise 19: The Tunnel	47
Exercise 20: The Horse	48
Exercise 21: The Aeroplane	49
Exercise 22: The World Upside Down	50
Exercise 23: The Somersault	52
Rope Games	54
Exercise 1	54
Exercise 2	56
Exercise 3	57

Exercise 4	58
Exercise 5	59
Exercise 6	60
Exercise 7	61
Exercise 8	62
Games with the Newspaper	63
Exercise 1	63
Exercise 2	64
Exercise 3	65
Exercise 4	67
Exercise 5	68
Exercise 6	70
Ball Games	72
Exercise 1	73
Exercise 2	74
Exercise 3	76
Exercise 4	77
Exercise 5	78
7 TO 12 -YEARS OLD	79
Games with the Body	79
Exercise 1: The Wheelbarrow ..	80
Exercise 2: The Table	81
Exercise 3: The Sculptor	82
Exercise 4: The Mirror	83
Exercise 5: The Swing	84
Exercise 6	85
Exercise 7: Standing Pulse	86
Exercise 8: Pulse on the Ground	88
Exercise 9	89
Exercise 10	90
Exercise 11	91
Exercise 12	92
Exercise 13: The Balance	93
Exercise 14	94
Exercise 15	95
Exercise 16	96
Exercise 17	97
Exercise 18	98
Rope Games	99
Exercise 1	99
Exercise 2	102
Exercise 3	103
Exercise 4	104
Exercise 5	105
Exercise 6	106

Ball Games	108
Exercise 1	108
Exercise 2	109
Exercise 3	110
Exercise 4	112
Exercise 5	114
Exercise 6	116
Exercise 7	117
Rope Games and the Ball	118
Exercise 1	118
Exercise 2	119
Exercise 3	120
Exercise 4	121
GROUP GAMES	123
Body-only Games	124
Exercise 1: Up and Down	124
Exercise 2: Listening and Go	125
Exercise 3: The Train and the Driver	126
Exercise 4: The Thieves and the Treasure	127
Exercise 5: Moving House	128
Exercise 6: The Signal	129
Exercise 7: The Word Key	130
Exercise 8: The Network	131
Exercise 9: The Cage	132
Exercise 10: Garments	133
Exercise 11: The Chicken Blind	134
Ball Games	135
Exercise 1: The Viper	135
Exercise 2: Air, Land, Sea	136
Exercise 3: Stop	137
Exercise 4: The Grasshopper	138
Exercise 5: Bears	139
Rope games	140
Exercise 1: Deer and Leopards	140
Exercise 2: Mirrors and Puppets	141
Exercise 3: Into the Sea, on the Shore	142
GLOSSARY	143

INTRODUCTION

Nowadays, it is increasingly difficult to find occasions for the children to play, but perhaps it is even more difficult to find appropriate games. This book is aimed at all those who want to discover the joy and fun of playing with the children but, above all, they want to provide them with the right stimuli so that, in addition to having fun, they can grow and strengthen. Through these simple gymnastic exercises the child can explore and get to know his body and give free rein to fantasy, creativity and imagination.

This book is created for children between one and twelve years of age, although it is intended for parents, educators, monitors and all those who are interested, in one way or another, to find approaches and propose the most appropriate games for their age.

GYMNASTICS AS A GAME

The purpose of these pages can be summed up in four words: to grow up playing. In this book, the reader will find simple games that can enrich children's motor experiences. We have to consider gymnastics within an educational process in which the playful aspect plays a central role because the child learns to grow through games.

In the game, according to Frochel's definition, *"the vital impulse of the personality which demands to be given and to be constituted is manifested; the whole inner world of the child with its needs, its tendencies, its ideas and feelings are made manifest... Through the total possession of living play, the child moves and completes himself"*.

A game is disinterested; its purpose is to have fun even before the satisfaction of winning; it is spontaneous and arises from the desire to play without necessarily having to *serve a purpose*; in fact, it can go beyond its mere eventuality and become a true way of living, learning, growing, experimenting and maturing; it is fun, effort and commitment to reach a goal through self-improvement and self-improvement.

The game is therefore a response to very specific needs: it satisfies children's curiosity since it is a way of learning to conquer what is not known and which continually raises new questions and further deepening; at the same time, it is a response to the need for self-esteem insofar as it helps to improve one's own abilities. The game, in short, is an opportunity to release physical and mental energies which at the same time stimulate and involve the child to get the best out of himself by coordinating all his faculties.

The game, moreover, requires a great deal of creativity and imagination not only for those who play but also for those who propose the games.

The characteristics of the games vary according to age: the first games are egocentric, solitary, oriented towards the discovery of oneself and, later, of the surrounding world; there are also more social games through which the child interacts with others.

PSYCHO-MOTOR DEVELOPMENT OF THE CHILD

The psycho-motor development of the child is a slow and complex process that is explained not only in the field of actual movement but involves globally every sphere of the personality; therefore, we can also speak of cognitive and social development as well as psychological development.

Motor skills are closely related to cognitive skills because it is precisely through the latter that the development of the central nervous system is promoted; it is therefore of fundamental importance to provide the child with the necessary stimuli to acquire good motor skills that can then be applied to intellectual operations that go beyond simple movement.

As can be seen from the following diagram, we can distinguish two types of abilities, psycho-motor and physical:

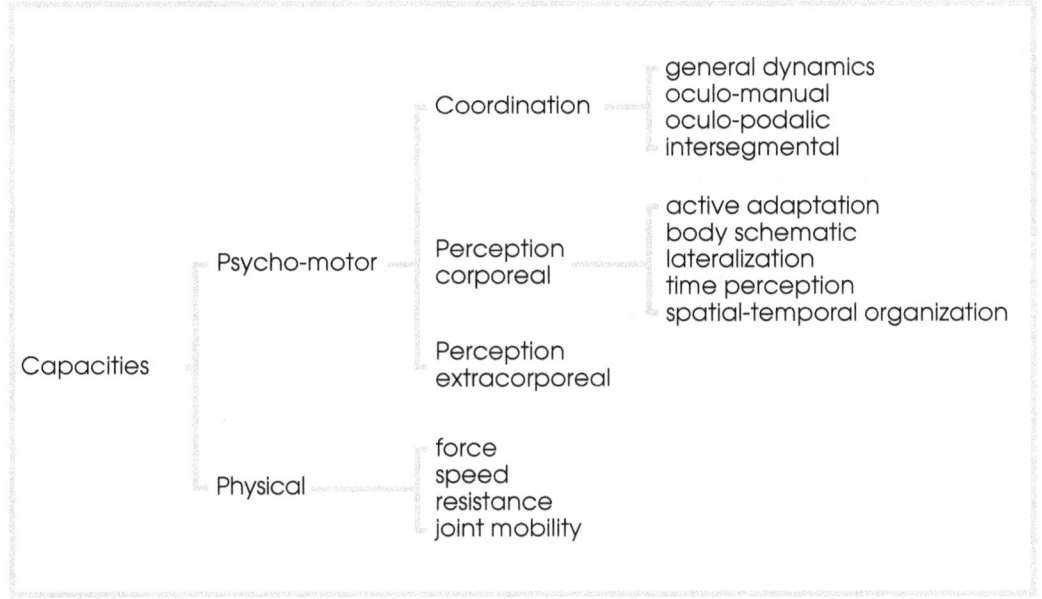

Psycho-motor skills

Psycho-motor skills, related to the central nervous system, can be classified into the following types:

> - coordination;
> - body perception in all its aesthetic and dynamic forms;
> - out-of-body perception (or spatio-temporal structuring).

Coordination

Coordination, according to K. Meinel's definition, is the *"harmonization of all partial processes of the motor act with respect to the goal to be achieved by the movement"*.

But there are more types of coordination: *general* coordination can be included in the above definition; *oculo-manual* coordination refers to the ability to coordinate hand and upper limb movements in relation to visual information; *oculo-podal* coordination is the ability to coordinate foot and lower limb movements in relation to visual information; *intersegmental* coordination is the ability to coordinate the movements of different body segments as regards the body, and *intersegmental* coordination is the ability to coordinate the movements of different body segments in relation to the body.

Important in the development of coordination are the sense organs, which receive very precise information of a tactile, acoustic, visual, vestibular, etc. type, transforming it into essential data for the process of controlling the motor act.

Body perception

Body perception is, according to J. Le Boulch's definition, "an overall intuition or immediate knowledge that we have of our body in a static position or in movement, in the relationship of the different parts to each other and in the relationships with the surrounding space, objects and people".

The child gets to know his own body and learns to use it through action; each new movement he makes is another experience that helps in a process that goes through very precise stages, starting from incoherent movements to the complete control of any gesture.

Within bodily perception we distinguish a number of functions:

Active adaptive function: the ability to rework acquired movements to be able to solve new situations and problems as they arise. The adaptive function develops from the first months of life until the age of ten or twelve; the greater the stimuli during this time, the greater the adaptive capacity with which the child's motor skills are enriched.

Body schema: it is structured from birth to reach its totality by the age of twelve, with the awareness of one's own body in each of its segments in static and dynamic situations, in relation to others and the outside world. The evolution of the body schema follows well-defined stages on the way to adulthood. In fact, we can distinguish four moments:

- that of the *patient body*, from birth to three months: motor skills are very elementary, consisting of reflexes and innate automatisms aimed at satisfying the child's own vital needs (sucking reflex, etc.);

- that of the *living body*, from three months to three years of age; this is a voluntary motor phase in which the first relationships are established between the different perceptual capacities (auditory, visual, tactile, etc.) and in which basic motor schemes such as running, jumping, balancing, climbing, etc. begin to be structured. In other words, the child recognizes his or her own body and knows how to insert it into the world around him or her;

- that of the *perceived body*, from the age of three to six years. The body becomes an object of great interest for the child: information from the body, which up to this point had remained unconscious, is now taken in consciously; at this stage, the child can internalize all the information and stimuli from his own body and the outside world and therefore to organize space (perceiving distances and dimensions) and also to become aware of his own body schema (knowing all its parts);

- that of the *represented body*, from the age of six to twelve: whereas before the child acted without mentally structuring the image of the movement he was about to perform, now he knows how to represent the gestures before performing them.

Lateralization: the child discovers which is his or her "preferred hand" and the dominance of one cerebral hemisphere over the other is reinforced. Until the child has achieved good lateralization, his body schema, the efficiency of his movements and his coordination will be imprecise and poorly organized.

Temporal perception: the ability to become aware of sound sensations with their duration and pauses. It helps the child in the development of motor coordination which is explained through a combination of movements that develop simultaneously or in succession in space and time.

Spatiotemporal organization: this is the ability to organize space, taking as presuppositions the concepts of above and below, in front and behind, right and left, referring to oneself and transferred to the outside world, putting it in relation to time.

Out-of-body perception

It allows us to know the external world and to structure it based on the concept of time and space and by making use of the functions of spatial organization and temporal perception already mentioned.

Physical capacities

Physical capacities are strength, speed, endurance and joint mobility. As far as strength, speed and endurance are concerned, we can say that they are poorly developed during childhood when motor skills require neither continuous strength actions nor speed or endurance performances.

Strength capacity improves markedly between the ages of three and five, while speed and endurance show a marked increase between the seventh and tenth year of life.

Joint mobility, on the other hand, is at its maximum during childhood and decreases, if not properly trained, as we approach adulthood; this is the capacity for maximum joint movement and depends on the extensibility of the muscles and ligaments.

Physical abilities also include balance, by which the body maintains or re-establishes a certain position. This requires not only the intervention of an anti-gravitational muscular action, but also sensory information such as visual, tactile, depth perception, laterality and verticality.

Two forms of equilibrium are distinguished: static equilibrium, when the body remains in a certain position, or dynamic equilibrium, when the barycentre finds its own verticality with respect to the base of support during the execution of any movement.

The ability to balance is closely related to body perception and therefore to the perfect knowledge of the positions assumed by the different body segments, in relation to themselves and to space.

From one to six years

After the first year of life, the child has conquered the upright position and has acquired the ability to walk.

During the first three years, the child learns forms of movement such as crawling, balancing, walking, climbing, jumping, pushing, pulling, climbing, hanging, carrying, swinging, as well as catching, one-handed and two-handed throwing movements.

These increasingly complex motor skills are explained in the way that the child finds most natural, i.e. through play and imitation.

The movements, up to the age of three years, are rather slow, limited in space and reduced in width, lacking that strength which will develop later, and accompanied, perhaps, by useless accessory movements.

Coordination skills are still rather coarse; in fact, the abilities to control, transform and adapt movement are underdeveloped.

During these years, the child needs to live in an environment that is as stimulating as possible and in which he/she can run, jump, hold on, balance, climb, etc.; in addition, the adult must stimulate the child's desire to play, to play imitation games by performing, if necessary, the movements that the child will copy and accompanying him/her with simple and immediate verbal indications.

After the age of three, the motor skills learned up to this point begin to be perfected. The forms of movement in which the greatest progress is generally noted are walking, running, climbing,

stretching, pushing, throwing, catching, turning and balancing. These movements can now even be combined: for example, if the child previously knew how to run and jump, he or she now knows how to insert jumping into the action of running.

As far as physical abilities are concerned, progress can be found in strength and speed, but above all in endurance and balance. Movements appear, therefore, faster and more energetic but, above all, broader, although they still reveal imperfections in fluidity and constancy.

Between the ages of four and six, the child needs to be always active and constantly busy; therefore, it is essential to give him/her the possibility to move and express him/herself freely, stimulating him/her to do better and better things.

From seven to twelve years old

Motor behaviour between the ages of seven and nine is characterized by a remarkable liveliness, accompanied by a readiness to face and solve new difficulties.

The child now learns to control his impulses and to concentrate his efforts on an activity in order to obtain the desired result. During this period, there is a noticeable increase in speed, endurance and the ability to combine movements, which become more fluid and reveal a good sense of rhythm.

In this phase, the child should be provided with as many stimuli as possible, diversifying the type of activity and always supporting his or her need to move.

Between the ages of ten and twelve, motor behaviour is characterized by an improvement in learning abilities; the strong need to move, which has accompanied the child's development, is now translated into a more controlled, rational and appropriate motor activity, characterized by curiosity and readiness to learn and to achieve new performances. The movement has now acquired a certain security, with the complete abandonment of useless accessory gestures. The child learns to coordinate his movements more and more in relation to himself (intersegmental, oculo-manual and podalicomanual coordination) and to the external world (spatial-temporal coordination).

This age is certainly the most profitable from the point of view of motor learning; the child, being extremely receptive, has to be stimulated as much as possible.

SOME TIPS BEFORE YOU START

The exercises proposed in this book are intended for an extremely young audience; we, therefore, believe that the direct intervention of an adult is indispensable, at least for the games aimed at children up to the age of six. In our case, we will refer to the mother, but it can also be the father, the babysitter, the teacher, etc. Consequently, the adult must also take an active part in the games; some are so simple that his or her job is only to provide some verbal indications, while others, more complex, require direct intervention.

When to do the exercises

These games can be proposed at any time of the day, when you have a little time to devote completely to your child, without interruptions.

It is essential to be eager to play and have fun, creating a deep and spontaneous complicity with the playmate. The child must also be predisposed; it is useless to propose games that involve him/her physically if he/she is tired and does not feel like playing.

There is no precise indication as to the frequency and duration of the exercises: they can be proposed once, twice, ten times in a week; they can be played for ten minutes or an hour, depending on your availability and until the child gets tired. Under no circumstances should we force them to play with us, but we must be skilful enough to be able to capture their attention.

Where to do the exercises

They can be carried out either indoors or outdoors.
Considering the difficulty of moving to open spaces such as parks, gardens or sports centres, we suggest playing at home, in as large a space as possible and on a non-slip surface.

Material required

The elements needed for the exercises are easy to locate; they are in fact:

> a skipping **rope**, preferably without a handle, used in rhythmic gymnastics, approximately 240 cm long and 7 or 8 mm thick, which can be bought in sports shops;
>
> any **newspaper**;
>
> **a foam ball** (25 to 30 cm in diameter) which can be bought in a toy or sports shops.

It is advisable to wear comfortable clothing, such as a tracksuit, which allows maximum freedom of movement.
If playing at home, thick socks can be worn; if outdoors a pair of trainers will be most suitable.

HOW TO DO IT
THE EXERCISES

The games are proposed in sequence, from the easiest to the most difficult, and are divided into two main groups corresponding to the first two chapters of the part of the book entitled "Ready to play!

The first is aimed at children between the ages of one and six: these are games that the child plays alone, with the help of an adult, or together with the same adult.

The second group of games, on the other hand, is aimed at older children between the ages of seven and twelve; these are games in pairs, in which two children play together without the direct intervention of an adult.

At the end, the chapter "Group games" illustrates some exercises that, while having the same purpose and the same characteristics as the previous ones, are suitable for a larger group of children, such as when our children's friends come over. For obvious reasons, these exercises are normally recommended for children over the age of four or five.

FROM ONE TO SIX YEARS

The first group starts with very simple games, which develop knowledge of oneself, of others and of space, imitation games in which the child takes on the role of an animal, or imitates actions; some games develop a sense of rhythm.

It then moves on to games in pairs, which refer to some basic motor schemes such as jumping, pushing, pulling, dragging, running, etc.; these games have no real progression and can be proposed in any order.

Finally, exercises with equipment are shown: we start by using the rope, which is used improperly (i.e. it is not used for jumping); jumping with the rope, in fact, is a rather complex action that brings into play the sense of rhythm, motor skills and various types of coordination that a child rarely possesses before the age of six.

The rope games proposed here are very simple and allow the child, who has to put his own body in relation to an external object, to perfect certain gestures such as dragging and letting himself be dragged, jumping, unhooking, stretching, etc.

This is followed by exercises with a newspaper, a simple *tool* to stimulate static and dynamic balance and to improve spatial perception (the ability to distinguish right from left, the concept of up and down) and the sense of rhythm.

It then moves on to games with a ball: their use presupposes the complete acquisition of complex coordinations such as oculo-manual (between the hand and the eyes) and oculo-podalic (between the feet and the eyes), and must therefore be proposed when the child can develop all the preceding exercises without difficulty.

SEVEN TO TWELVE YEARS OLD

The second group of exercises also foresees a didactic sequence that follows certain stages; the child can already play with a partner who is more or less the same age as him/her.

The games are played in pairs and aim to improve different types of coordination and consolidate body perception, posture, balance, rhythm and strength.

We then move on to exercises that involve the use of apparatus: the rope, thanks to which it is possible to stimulate balance skills, and the ball, which brings coordination skills into play in an increasingly complex way. These two apparatuses are then used together, thus creating situations that require the ability to coordinate different movements in an increasingly complex way.

The ability to throw and catch a ball that rolls and bounces indicates a motor maturity that can be reached slowly. There is, therefore, no need to be surprised if the use of this tool is difficult and sometimes even boring for the child.

Motor development follows very precise stages on the way to adulthood, but each child has his or her own time and this has to be respected; therefore, each child has to be stimulated according to his or her own abilities but also has to be continuously stimulated to do better.

The greater the stimuli provided to the child, the greater the child's ability to adapt to them and therefore to learn.

READY TO PLAY!

FROM ONE TO SIX YEARS

GAMES WITH THE BODY

Games with the body do not require the use of any tools and are therefore, the easiest to understand and carry out. They can be done by the child alone, with the help of the mother, or even with the mother, who becomes an indispensable playmate.

The osteo-articular and muscular structure of the child allows him to move as he wishes, without risk (although the games could be painful for the mother, especially for her back and knees). It is therefore advisable not to try to do more than is possible and to proceed with caution when carrying out movements (in particular with regard to the frog and elephant exercises), especially when they are painful.

The so-called *imitation games*, in which a role is played, a character is acted out or an action is simply performed, are very useful and fun for children. Through these games, children develop their own sociability, give free rein to their imagination and also learn to move and express themselves through movement.

Imitation exercises should be preceded by a title that allows the exercise itself to be quickly identified and stimulates the child's imitative capacity, helping him/her to represent even mentally the gesture, object or animal that he/she is about to perform.

Exercise 1

The adult addresses the child by saying: "Show me how you put your hands over your ears.' The same can be repeated with other parts of the body, such as the eyes, knees, buttocks, feet, nose, etc. The exercise makes it possible to make each part of the child's body verbally and physically known to the child, who thus becomes able to perceive its existence.

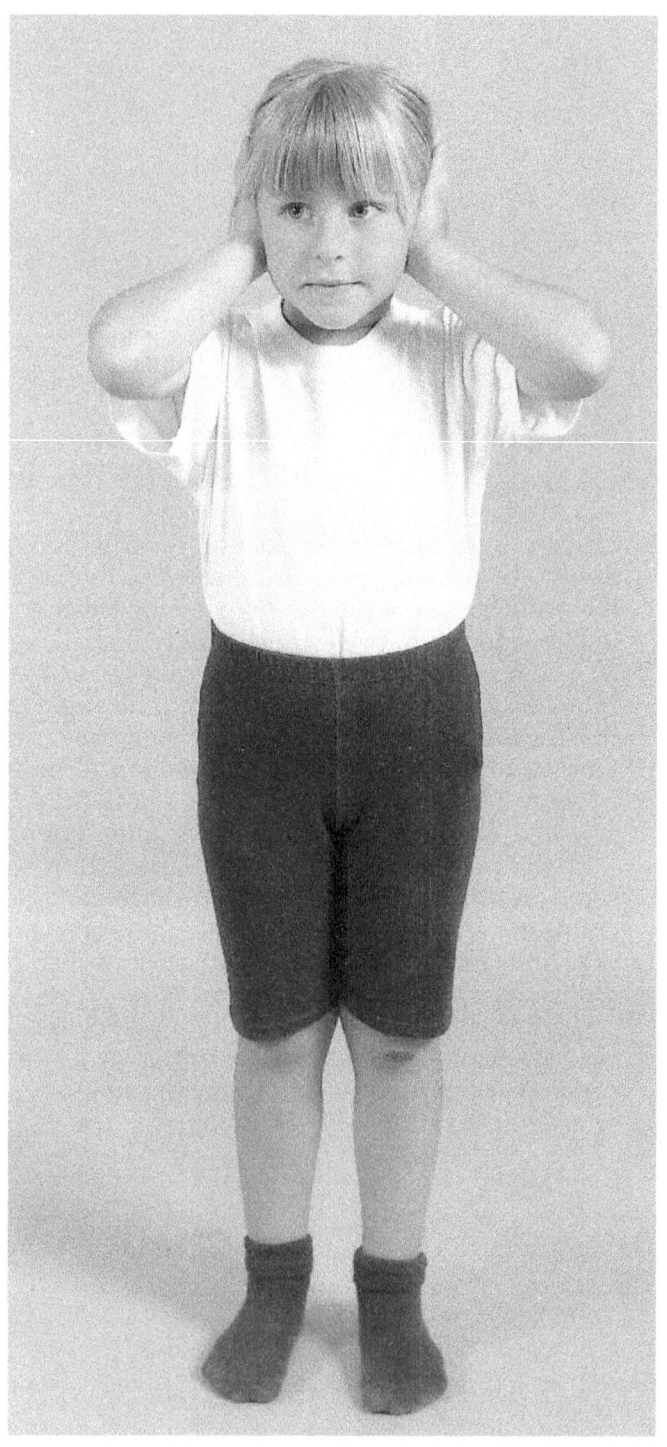

Exercise 2

When the child recognizes the parts of her body, she can be asked to point out the same parts on the mother's body, who addresses the child in the following way: "Show me how you put your hands over my ears.' When the child has acquired the knowledge of the different parts of the body about himself, we ask the child to perform the step that allows him to transfer the knowledge about himself learned so far to another person, thus shifting the child's own attention from himself to the outside world.

Exercise 3

The elephant

"Let's make the elephant," says the mother, inviting the child to bend forward with the trunk, placing the palms of the hands down near the feet and the arms stretched out to represent the trunk.

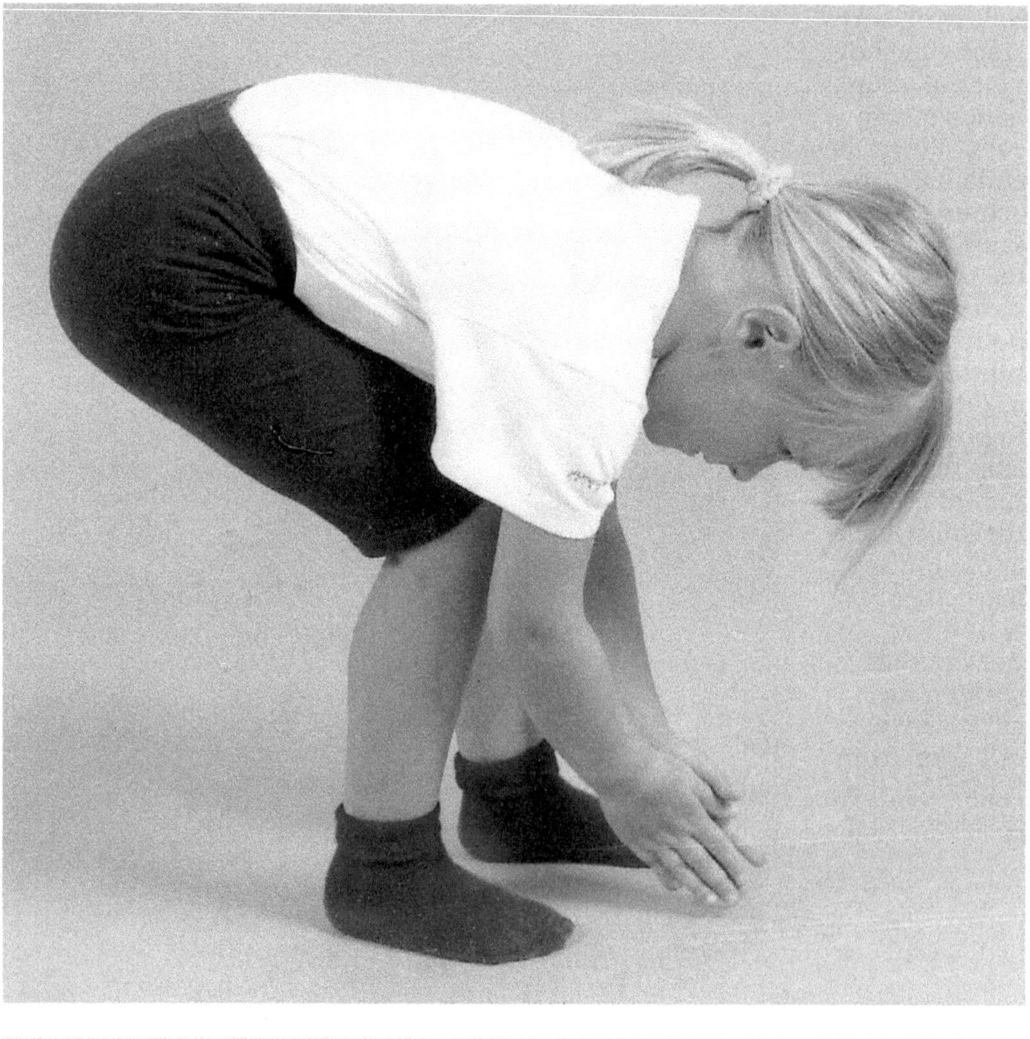

Exercise 4

The frog

"Let's make the frog," says the mother. The child will imitate her with feet apart, knees bent and hands resting on the floor in front of the feet, preparing to jump forward.

Exercise 5

The puppet

"Let's make the puppet," says the mother, inviting the child to imitate the movements of the puppets, moving his arms and legs with strokes and maintaining a certain rigidity of the trunk.

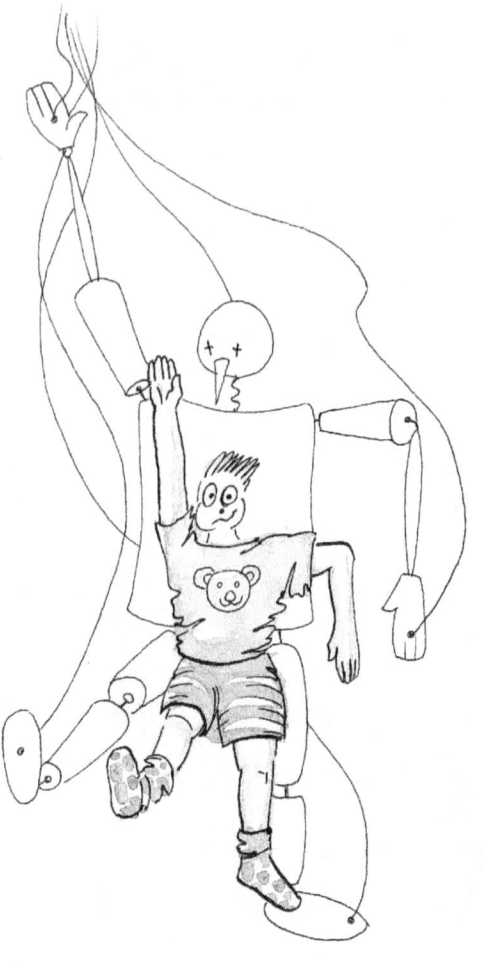

Exercise 6

The tree

"Let's imitate a windswept tree," says the mother, inviting the child to stretch his legs and put his feet together to imitate the trunk, while raising his arms and moving them as if they were branches shaken by the wind.

Exercise 7

The awakening flower

"Let's make the flower that wakes up in the morning," says the mother, inviting the child to get into a tucked-up position, with legs bent and trunk and head bent. From this position, the child stands up, progressively spreading his arms, back and legs apart and bringing his arms (the petals) outwards.

Exercise 8

The flower that falls asleep

The child has to perform the same movements as in the previous exercise but reversing the sequence.

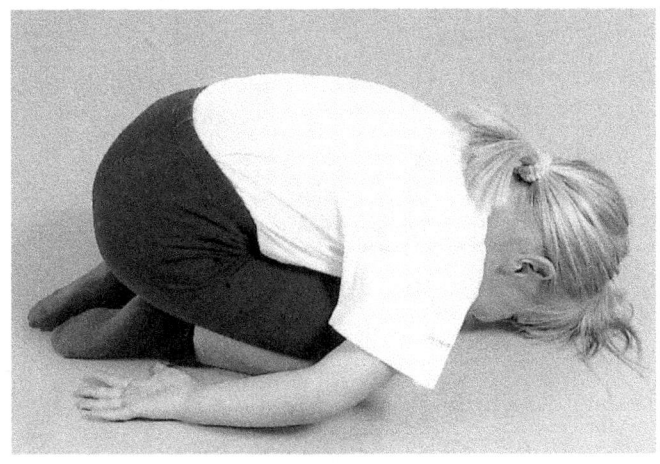

Exercise 9

Driving nails

"Let's make it look like we're hammering in a nail," says the mother, reaching forward with one arm as she bends over and holds out the other.

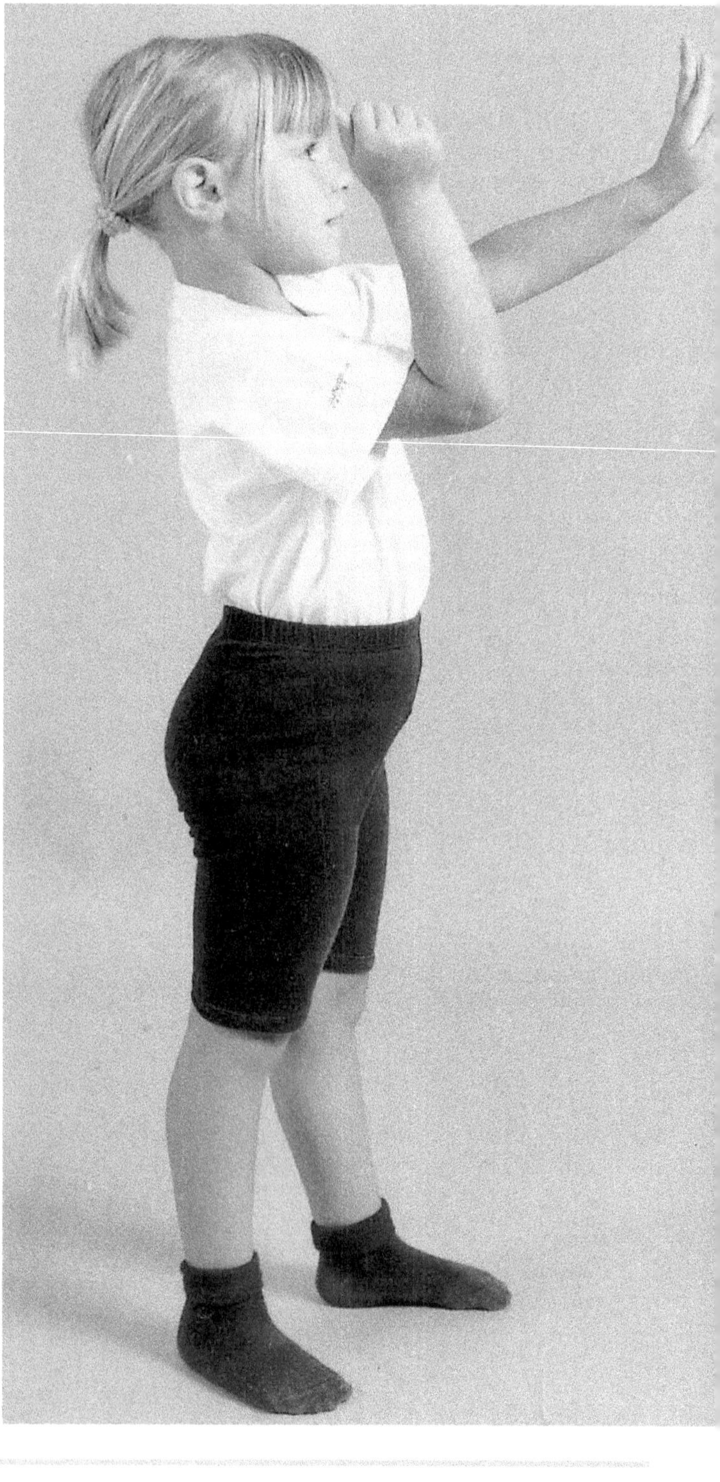

Exercise 10

The Indian and the cavalry

"Let's imitate the Indians who listen with their ear to the ground to hear if the cavalry is coming," says the mother, inviting the child to kneel down, pretending to hear the sound of horses.

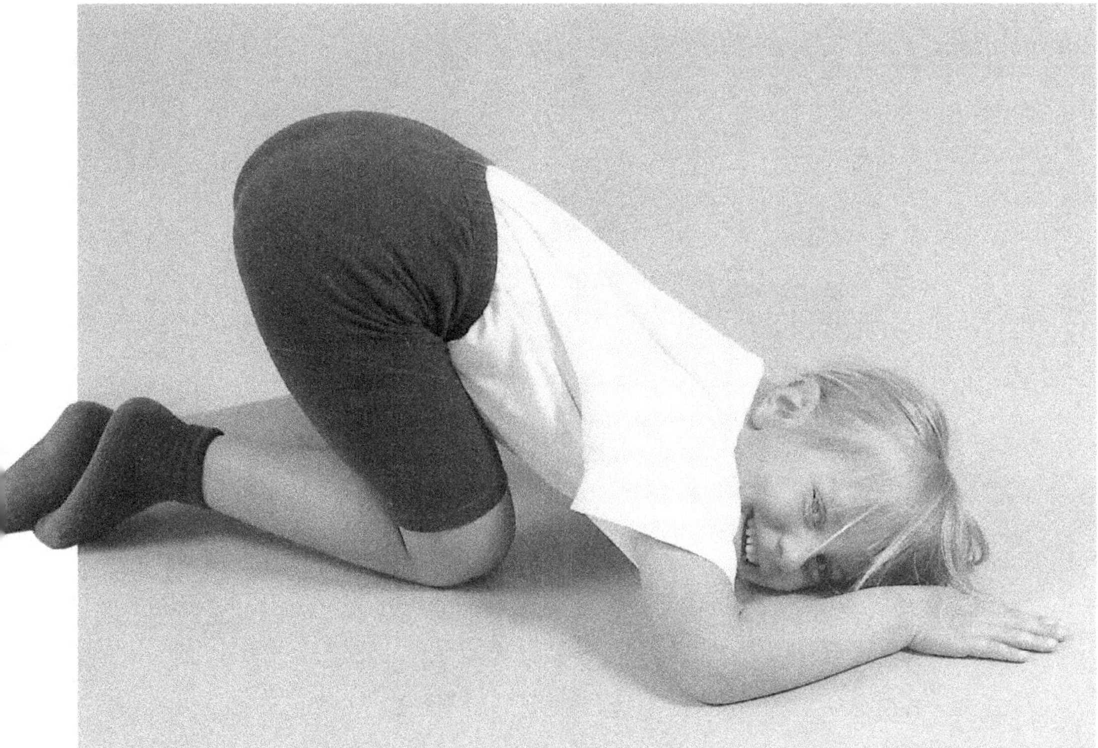

Exercise 11

The mother asks the child to walk and to clap her hands when she places each foot on the ground. In this way, the child learns to perceive the movement of his own body while walking and, in particular, of his own foot at the exact moment when it touches the ground, relating it to a sound sensation produced by himself (the clap): he has to perform two movements (footrest and clapping) that produce a sound effect in a coordinated way.

Exercise 12

The child walks freely; when its mother claps her hands, it stops on one foot.

When he claps his hands twice, he stops on one hand and one foot.

This simple exercise also brings into play the sense of rhythm, as well as the balance necessary to maintain a stable position.

The sound sensation is not produced by the child himself as in the previous exercise but comes from the outside; for this reason, he will have to be very attentive to the clapping he will hear, as he has to combine an auditory sensation with a gesture that occupies him from the point of view of coordination and balance.

Exercise 13

The Traffic Light

The mother explains to the child that each colour of the traffic light corresponds to a movement: she mentions the different colours and invites the child to perform the corresponding action.

For example:

Green = Walking
Yellow = Running
Red = Stop

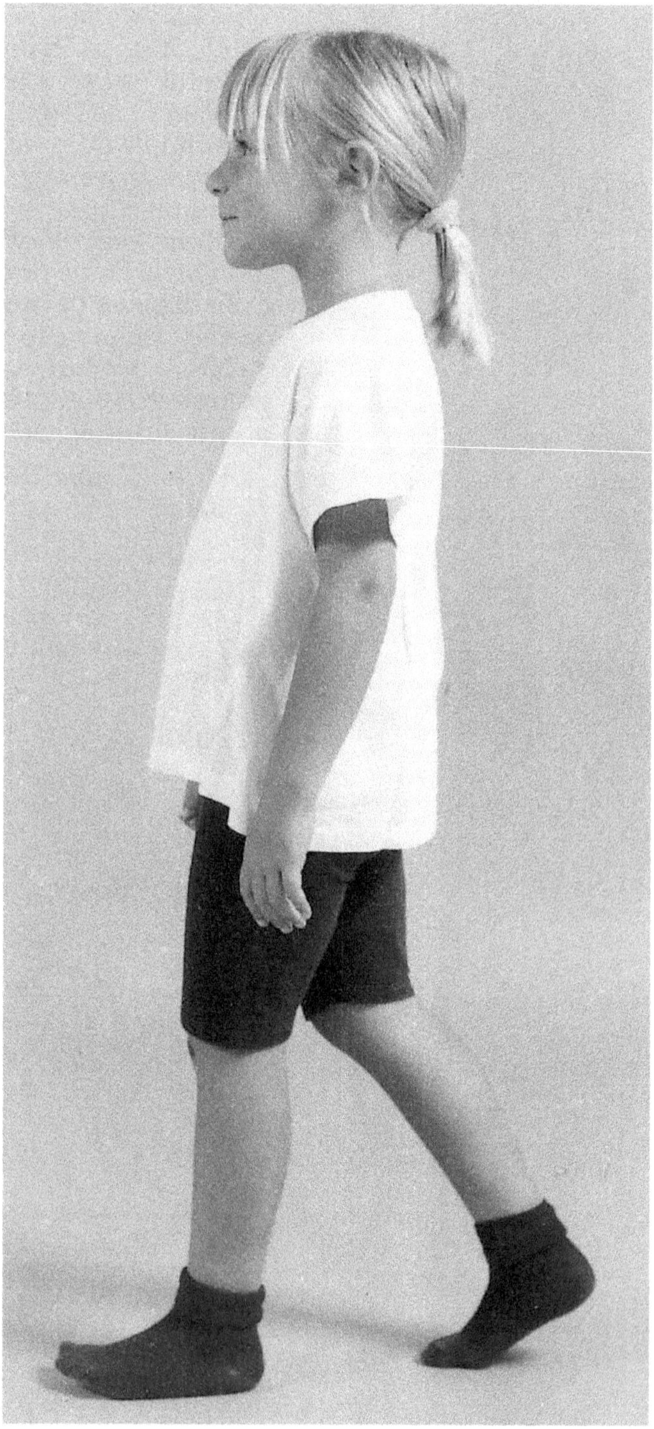

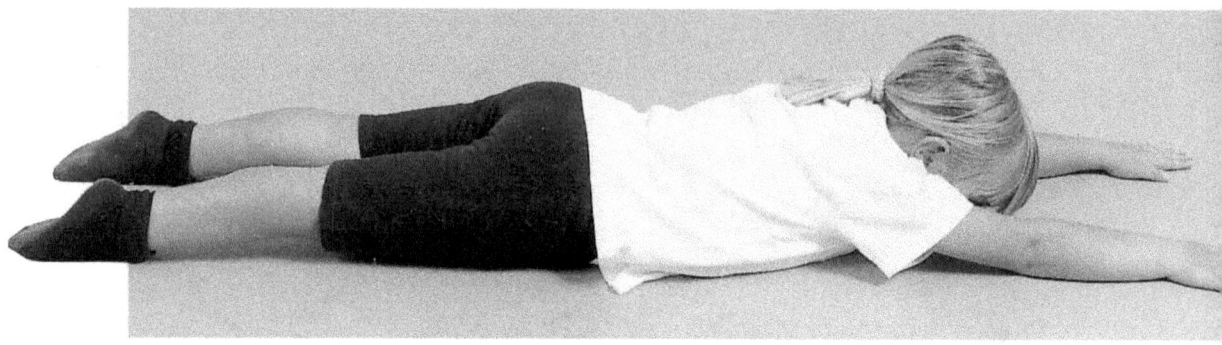

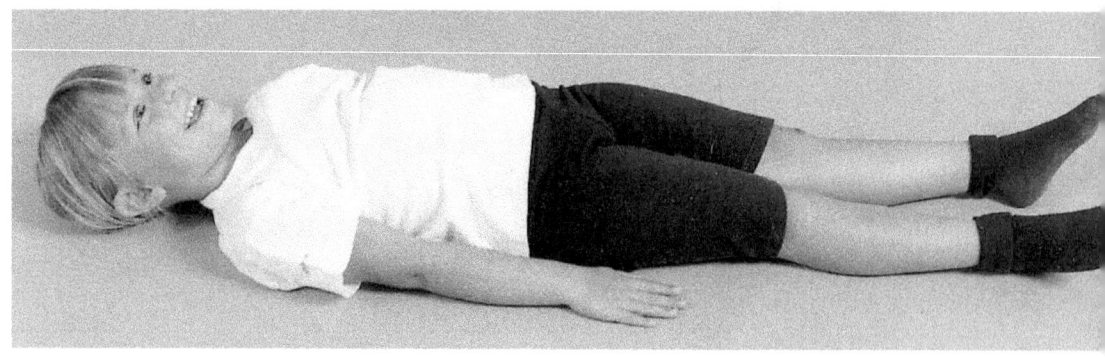

Or also:
Green = Prone;
Yellow = Supine;
Red = Sitting.

Or also:
Green = Running;
Yellow = Stop on one foot;
Red = Sit down.

In this way, the child is stimulated to create a mental image of the action to be performed (whether it is walking, running or stopping) by relating it to a verbal indication. The same game can be played by replacing the colours of the traffic light with another type of verbal indication, such as, for example, names corresponding to different actions:
Mary = to walk;
John = to run;
Francis = to stop.
Or with an audible indication:
One clap = prone;
Two claps = supine;
Three claps = sitting.

Exercise 14

The Tightrope Walker

The child stands on something (chair, step, suitcase) and balances on one foot.
The use of something to stand on makes this simple exercise, which requires good balance in a static situation, a little more complicated.

Exercise 15

The Tightrope Walker who Goes Up and Down

The child climbs up and down with the back to something (chair, step, suitcase).

In this way, the child is asked to perform a coordinated gesture: when walking backwards, he is not able to see the object he is climbing over, nor the ground he is descending to, and he will be very attentive to tactile sensations coming from the support of the foot. The attention and coordination required to contribute to the child's construction of the body schema.

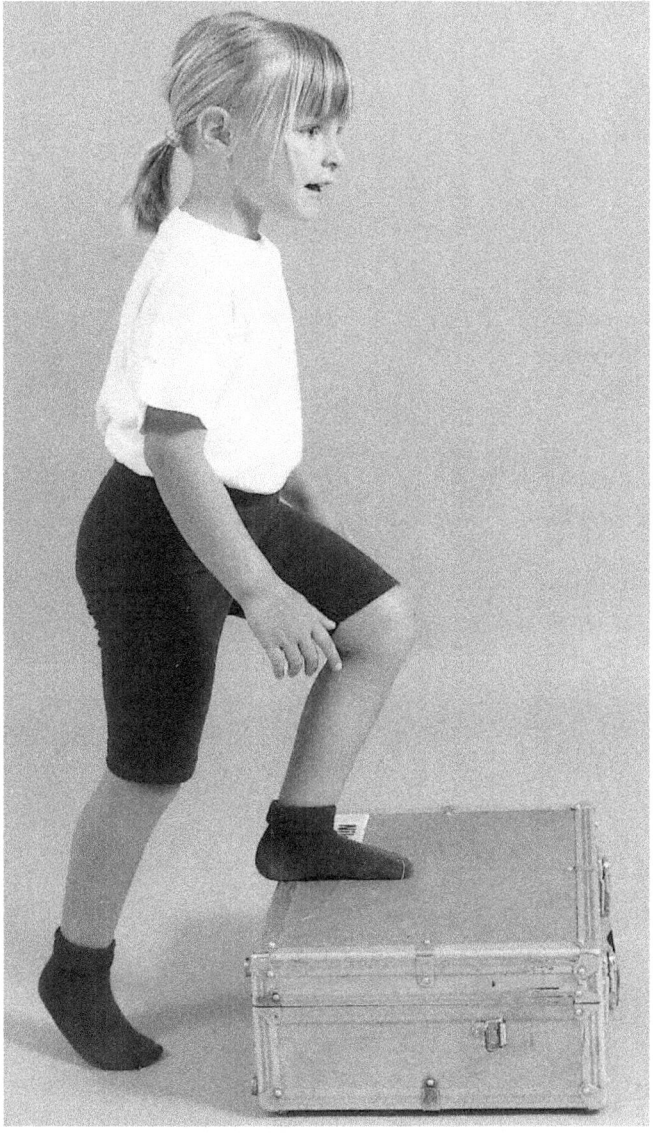

Exercise 16

The mother lies as low to the ground as possible. She asks the child to step over her. The same game can be played by reversing the roles. Through this exercise, the basic scheme of overcoming an obstacle comes into play.

Exercise 17

The Tree Trunk

The child imitates a log, stretched out on its back with its arms raised: the mother takes him by the hands and drags him along.

The same game can be played by reversing the roles; the mother will then have to help the child by pushing with her feet.

Through this game, the active and passive crawling motor scheme is activated, allowing the child to develop his or her strength.

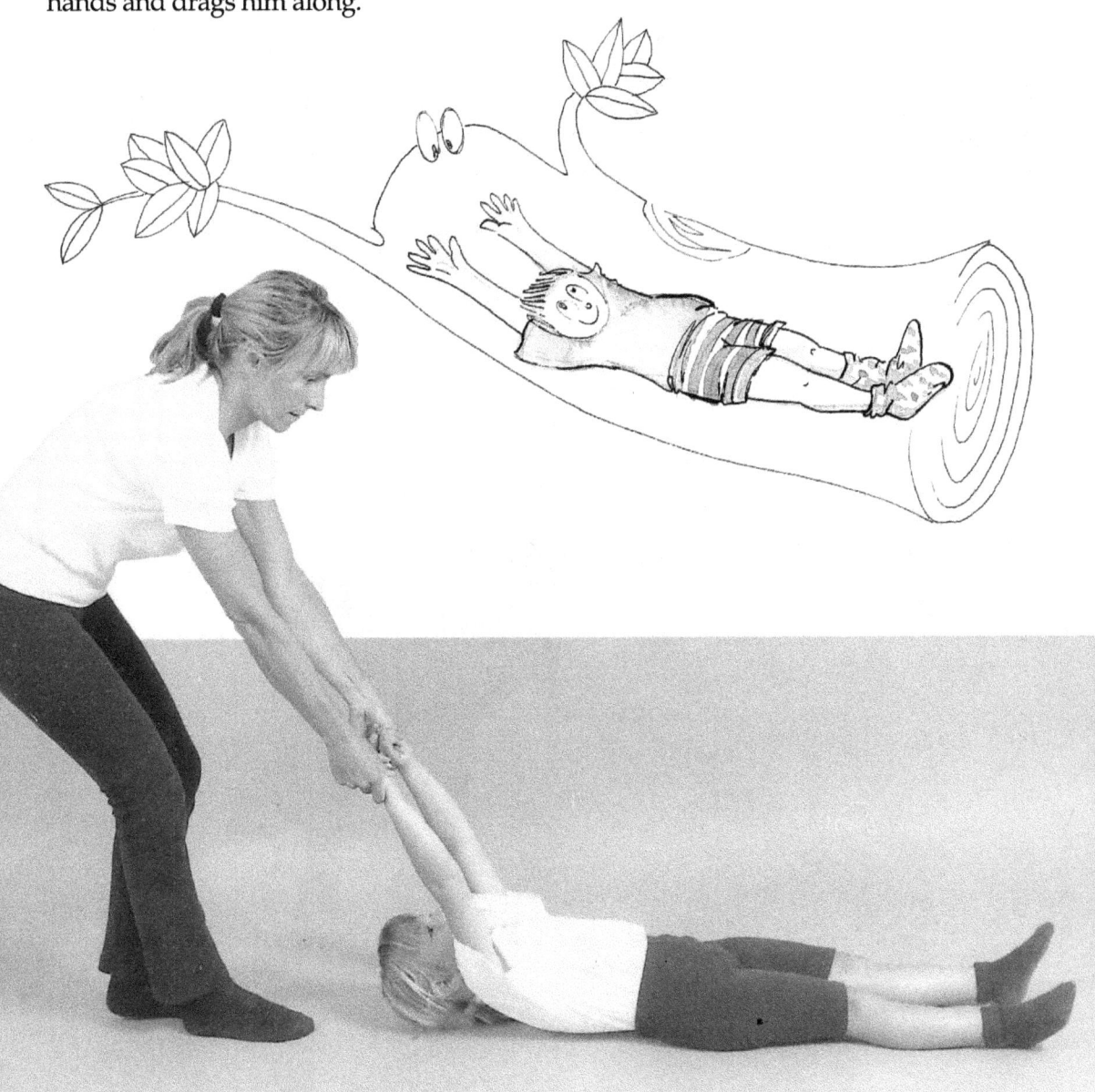

Exercise 18

The mother lies on her stomach on her hands with her arms straight and on her feet with her legs straight: the child must try to make her fall by pushing her down from behind.
It is a game of strength in which, although the child is unlikely to defeat his mother on his own, his mother will have to give in to his efforts.

Exercise 19

The Tunnel

The mother lies on her stomach as in the previous exercise but with her hips more raised (see exercise 18) and with her legs apart; the child *imitates the train* passing under his mother on one side, on the other side and between her legs. The child moves in this case as it wishes, walking or crawling; in this way, it learns the concepts of above and below, in front and behind, and right and left.

Exercise 20

The Horse

The mother stands on all fours but on her back, with her legs bent and her body in a horizontal position. The child stands on top of the mother as if she were a horse. This game, in addition to amusing the child and creating a certain complicity with the mother, helps the child to learn to maintain balance in particular situations.

Exercise 21

The Aircraft

The mother lies on the floor, face up, with her legs bent over her chest; the child rests with its trunk on the mother's legs, who holds it by the hands to keep it balanced. This game creates a certain complicity between mother and child, who learns to maintain balance even in unstable situations.

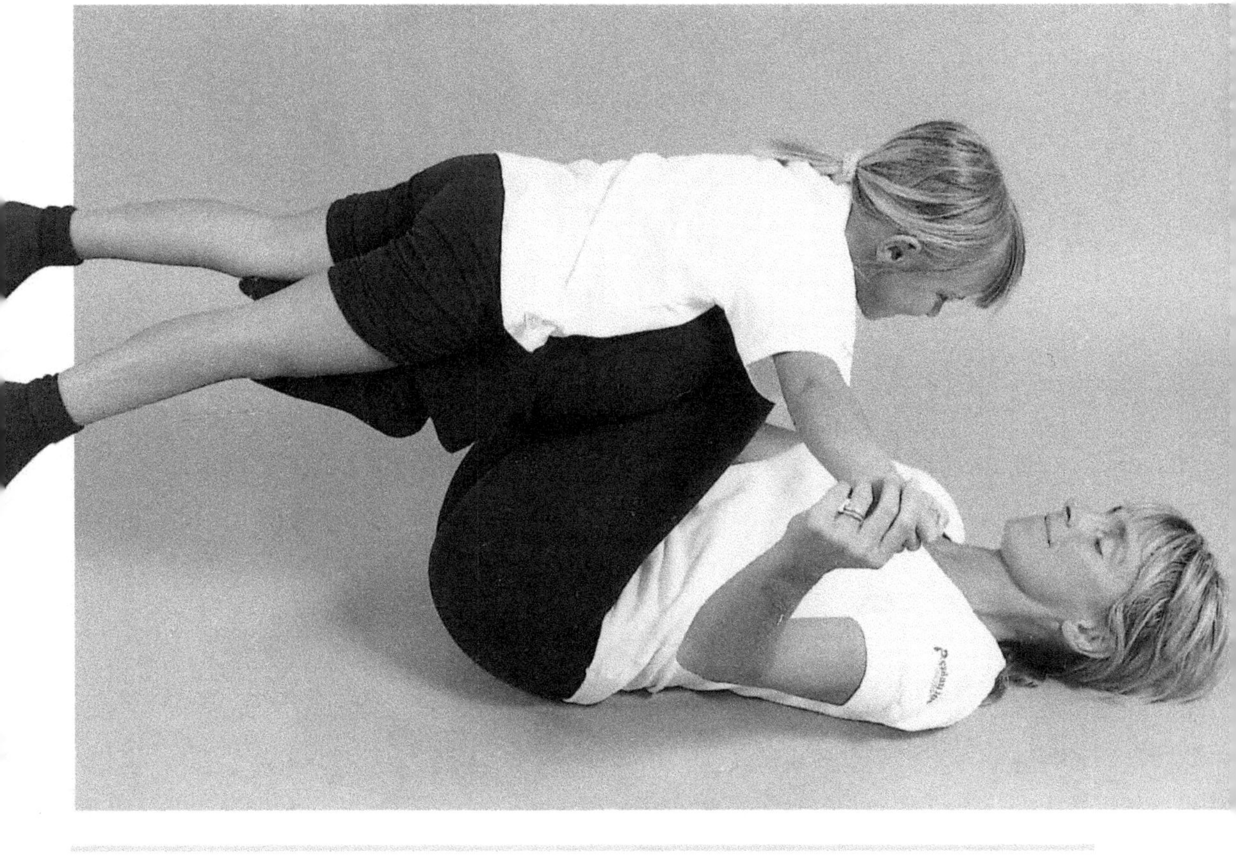

Exercise 22

The World Upside Down

The mother, standing, holds the child's ankles so that she can support her child on the floor with her hands, remaining upright.

The child then has to take small steps with his hands in the direction of the mother's feet, passing under her legs until he passes over them and then back again, always held by the mother.
From the vertical position, the world around the child appears upside down. He finds himself in a new situation in which he must have perfect control of his own body, trying to remain rigid so as not to fall. This requires good balance but, above all, perfect spatial perception, thanks to which the movements of the child's own body can be coordinated in relation to space.
It has to walk in the direction of its mother's feet and back, always with small steps on its hands, thus learning to coordinate its body movements even when it is upside down.

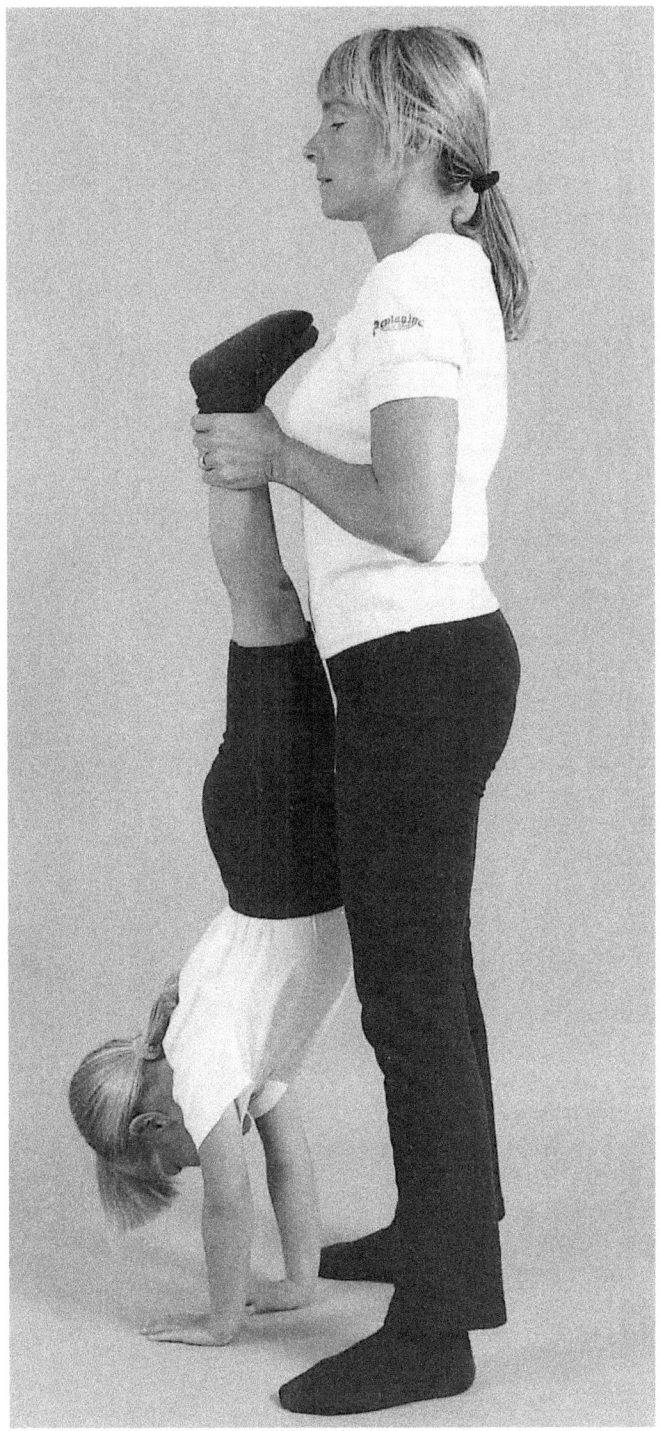

Exercise 23

The Somersault

The mother and child are standing facing each other, holding hands. The mother has her legs slightly bent and spread apart.
The child rests one foot on the mother's thigh. Then the other foot is placed on the other leg and the trunk until the child pushes himself to turn around. Finally, the child performs a backward somersault, landing with his/her feet on the ground and always holding on to the hands.
Through this game, the child has to show a certain strength and courage to be able to hold on and overcome the initial fear that may arise when turning completely around, even though he is held by the mother. In this situation, too, the world appears *upside down* for a moment and also changes continuously as the child's position changes. In this way, the child learns to perceive the movements of the body even when it is turning on itself.

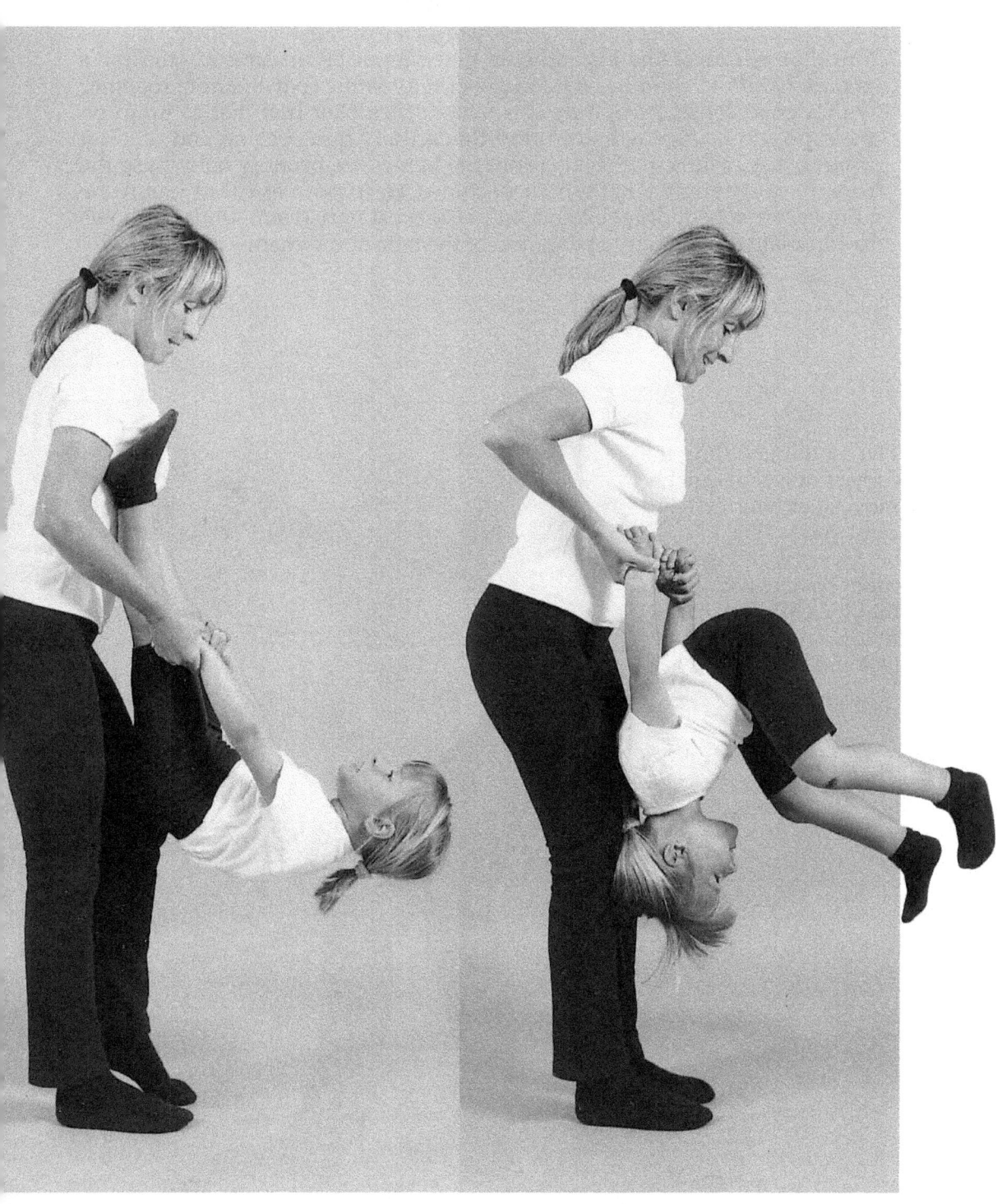

ROPE GAMES

The rope is one of the instruments that cannot be missing in children's games. Until the child has a good general dynamic coordination, together with a good sense of rhythm, it is very difficult for him/her to jump on the rope and he/she will even find this activity quite boring and will not achieve any results. For this reason, the games we propose below use the rope in a different way, which becomes an instrument that has to be jumped, stretched, dragged and hit in the most varied situations; it allows to stimulate the capacity of balance, both static and dynamic.

Exercise 1

The mother, holding the rope at one end, quickly moves her hand left and right and walks backwards, giving the rope the effect of a snake that the child has to follow and catch with his feet and hands.

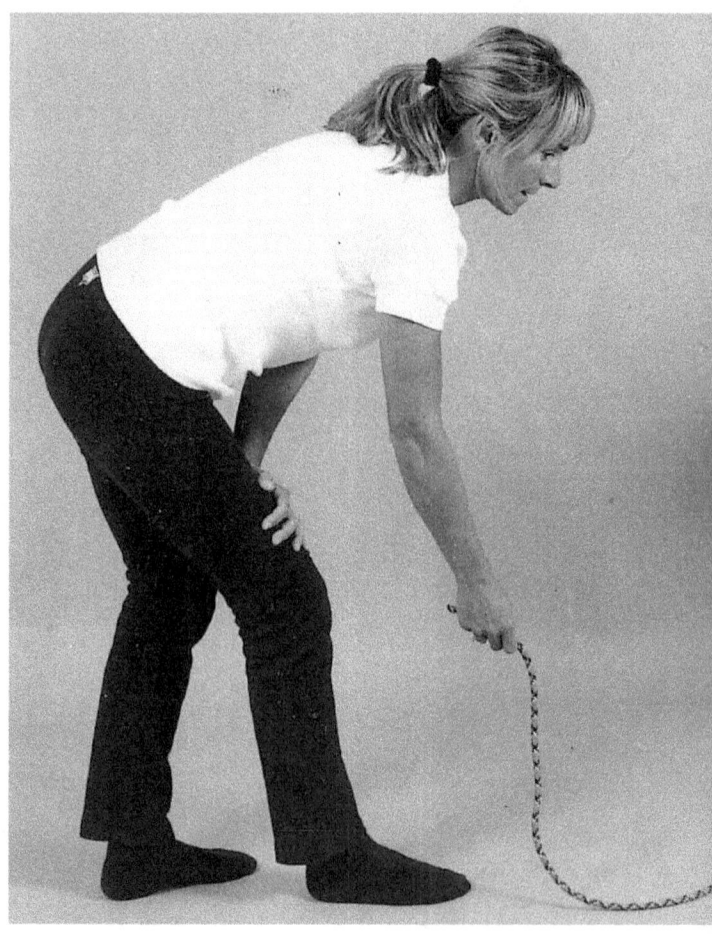

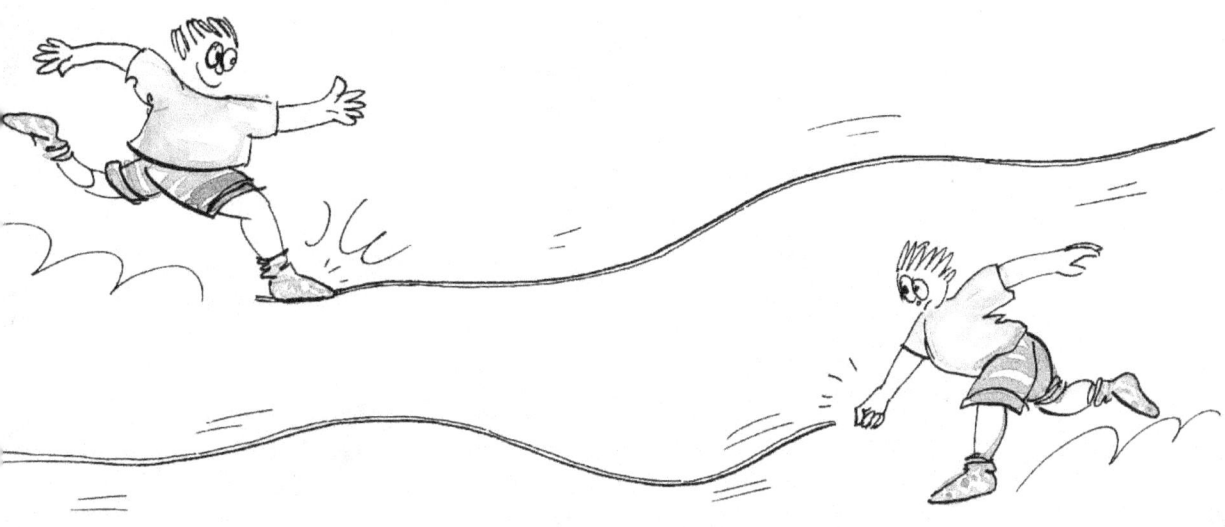

The same exercise can be done by reversing the roles.
This is a simple game that allows the child to work on coordination in general: the child has to concentrate attention on the movement of the rope, anticipating the movement and moving the feet or hands when appropriate.
Therefore, it must have a clear idea of the space occupied by the rope (spatial organization) and the time in which it moves (temporal perception): in addition, it has to relate the spatial organization and the temporal perception to the movement it will have to make in order to step on the rope.

Exercise 2

The mother holds the ends of the rope with both hands, while the child, who has his back to her, holds the rope around his belly and walks forward to stretch his mother, who puts up a little resistance.
The same exercise can be done by reversing the roles.
This exercise clearly brings into play the motor scheme of pulling and dragging.

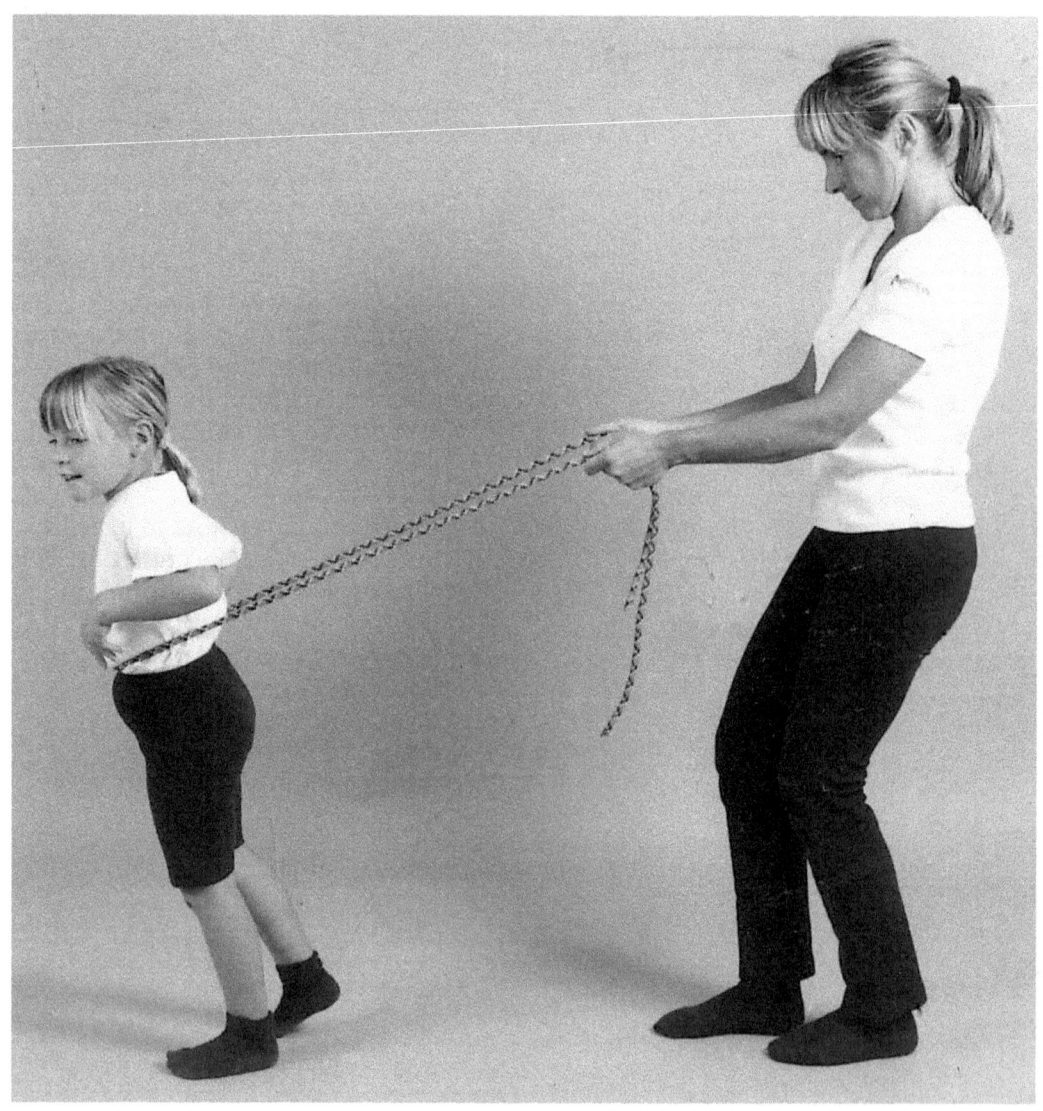

Exercise 3

The mother and child, facing each other, hold the rope; the child walks backwards trying to pull the mother, who will put up minimal resistance. Then the roles will be reversed and it will be the mother who pulls.
Also in this exercise, the motor schema of dragging comes into play; the child is faced with an opposition to be confronted and this stimulates it to exert greater force in an attempt to counteract the mother.
The mother, in turn, can help by pulling the child towards her so that he can experience the motor schema of being pulled and realise his own capacity for strength.

Exercise 4

The rope is stretched out on the ground; the child walks on it with his feet on top of it, being careful not to lose his balance.
This exercise can also be performed by walking backwards.
The child must maintain balance while resting his or her feet on a small surface that does not allow him or her to move freely.
Walking backwards the situation becomes more complex because the child does not see where the foot rests and is stimulated to concentrate on the tactile sensations provided by the support of the foot itself.

Exercise 5

Mother and child face each other and hold hands; feet are on the rope (one in front of the other) and the front leg bent; and, pushing and pulling, each tries to pull the other off the rope.

This exercise brings into play the ability to balance in a static situation together with the ability to exert force.

Exercise 6

Mother and child face each other, with the rope stretched out on the floor between them. They push each other with their palms touching: the winner is the one who manages to get over the rope.
In this game, the child works on the capacity of strength and the motor scheme of pushing: the mother must let herself be won over by the child, but with a certain amount of resistance.

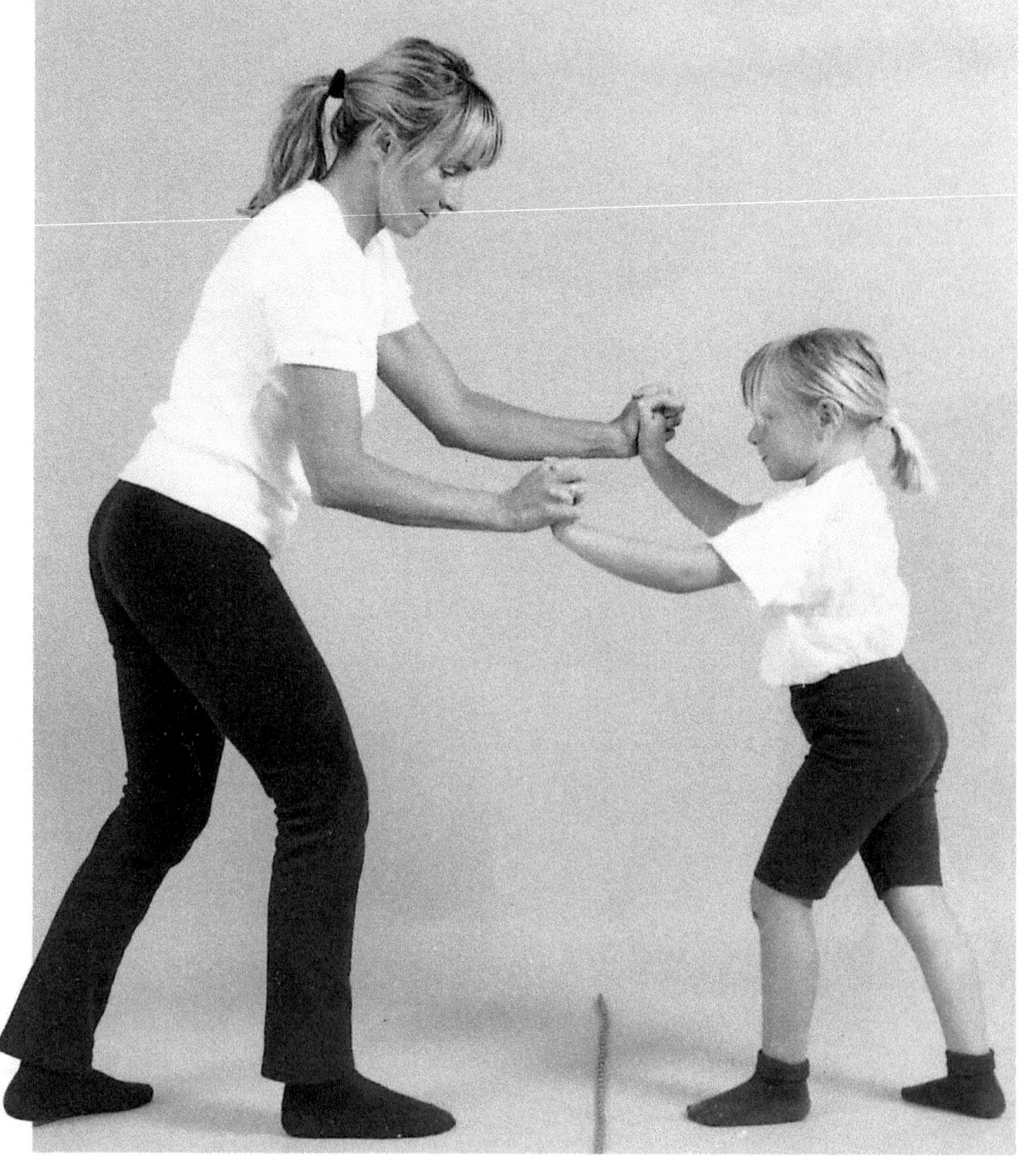

Exercise 7

Mother and child face each other and shake hands. Contrary to the previous exercise, here the mother and child pull on each other: the one who touches or overcomes the rope loses.
In this game, strength and the motor scheme of stretching are put to the test: the mother, being necessarily stronger, must at first let herself be won over by the child.

Exercise 8

The rope is tied at one end to a support (table leg, chair, etc.) and the other end is held by the mother: the child must pass under the rope without touching it, changing position as the mother lowers the rope.

Through this game, the child learns to value space and, above all, the space occupied by his own body in movement; in the attempt to pass under an obstacle, he learns to distinguish the concept of above and below, putting it in relation to the capacity for spatial organization.

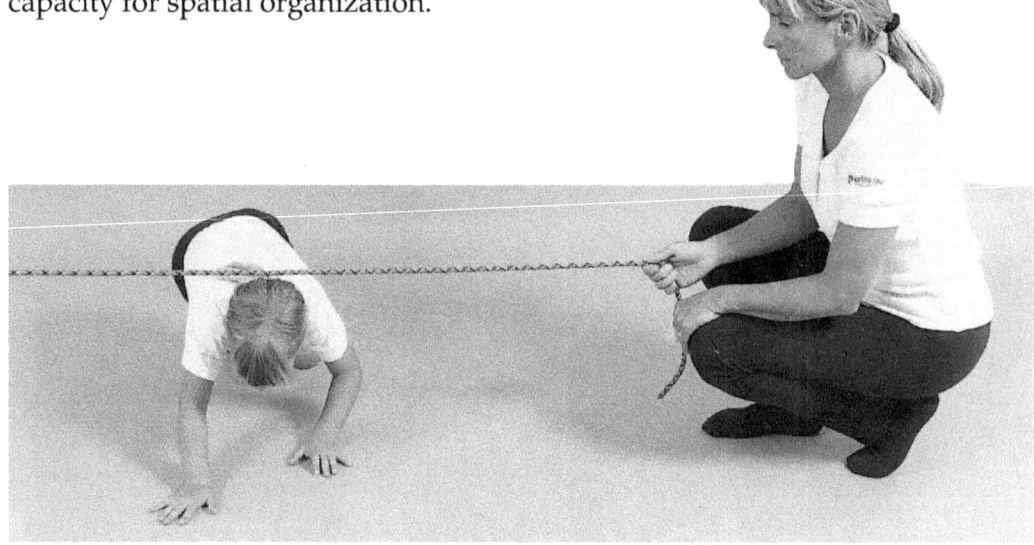

GAMES WITH THE NEWSPAPER

Although we cannot consider it a real instrument, the choice of the newspaper is not accidental and has some advantages: it is easy to find, it can be of different sizes depending on whether it is folded or not, it can be replaced if it breaks and it costs little. It allows for games that stimulate the sense of balance but also and above all games to consolidate spatial perception and therefore the concepts of above and below, in front and behind, right and left, etc.

Exercise 1

The child lies on the floor, face up, on all fours with the newspaper on his belly. The child must move without the newspaper falling.
This is a simple game that stimulates the ability to balance in a situation made more complex by the presence of an unstable object.

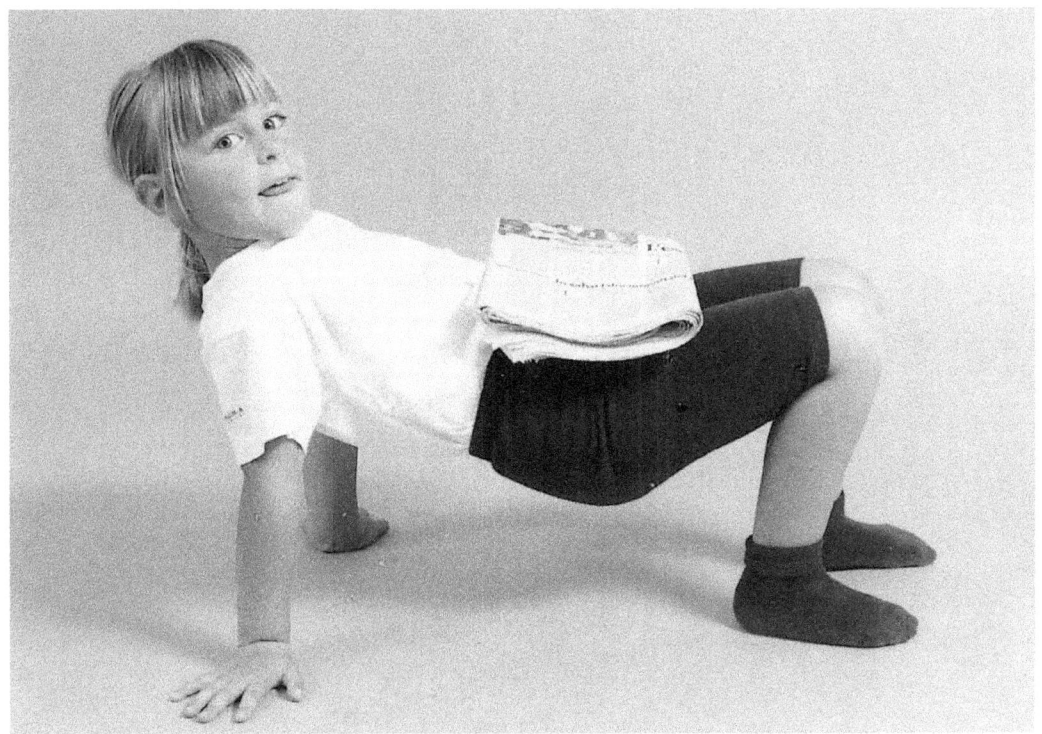

Exercise 2

The child carries the newspaper on his head and walks trying not to let it fall. This is a rather complicated situation for the child as he has to perform a movement, such as walking while trying to keep the rest of his body still: the ability to balance and body perception is particularly stimulated here.

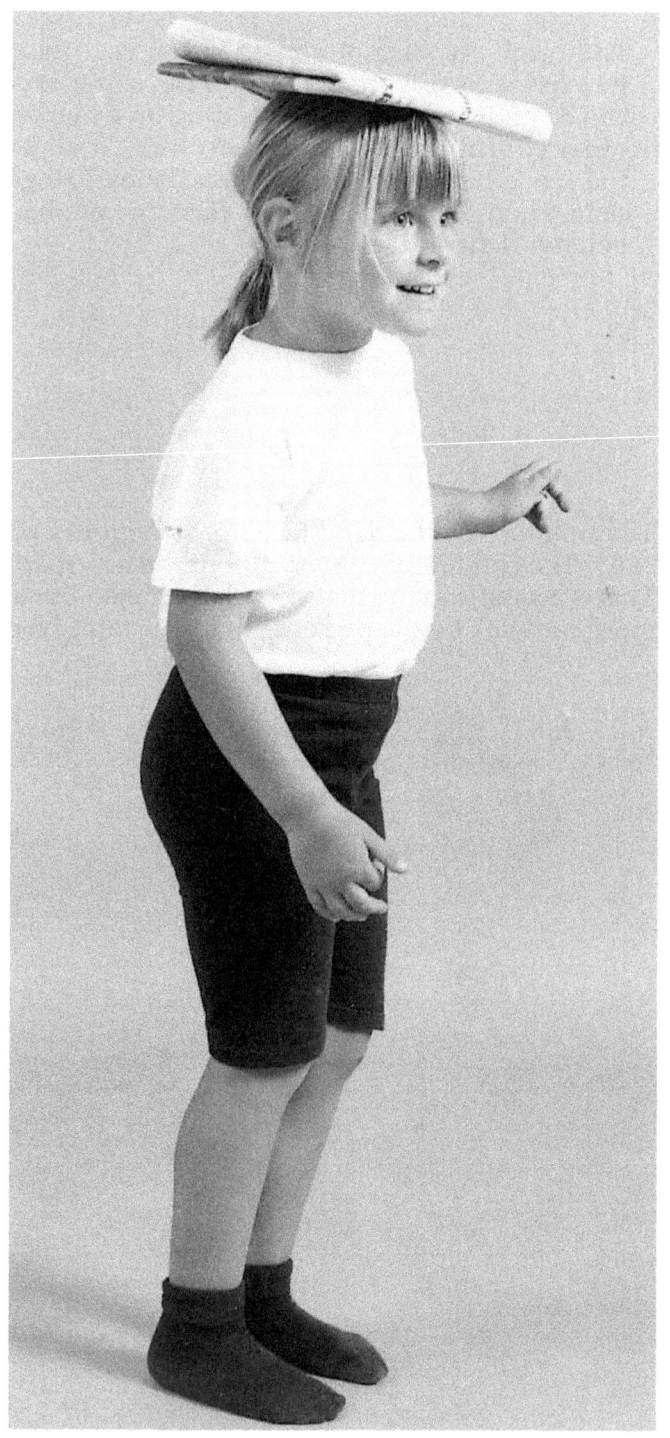

Exercise 3

The newspaper, folded, is placed on the floor; the child has to stand on it and balance by choosing three points of support.
To begin with, the child must balance on two feet and one hand.

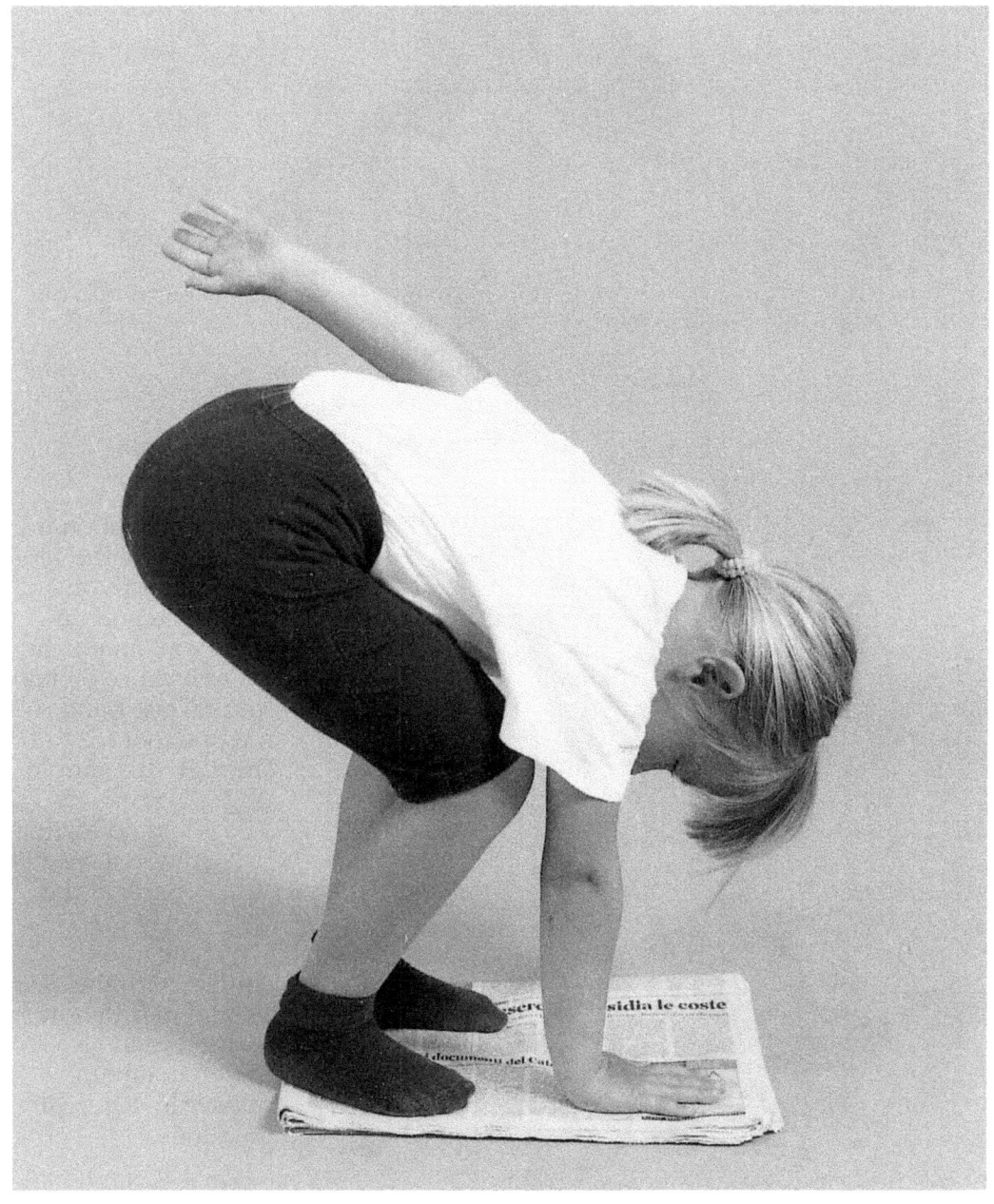

Then the position is changed and the child balances on two hands and one foot. And, finally, he has to balance on his bottom, one hand and one foot.
Through this simple game, the child learns about the parts of the body that come into contact with the ground in different positions and also how to maintain balance in different situations.

Exercise 4

The sheets of newspaper are placed one behind the other, slightly separated to the right and left; the child jumps from one sheet to the other with the right foot on the right and the left foot on the left, taking care not to step directly on the floor. This is an exercise that presupposes a good capacity for spatial organization together with the acquisition of the concepts of above and below and right and left in relation to oneself (right foot to the right and left foot to the left) and to space. Here the child has to coordinate jumping movements by calculating the distance to be covered, the space occupied by his feet on the sheets and the space occupied by the sheets themselves.

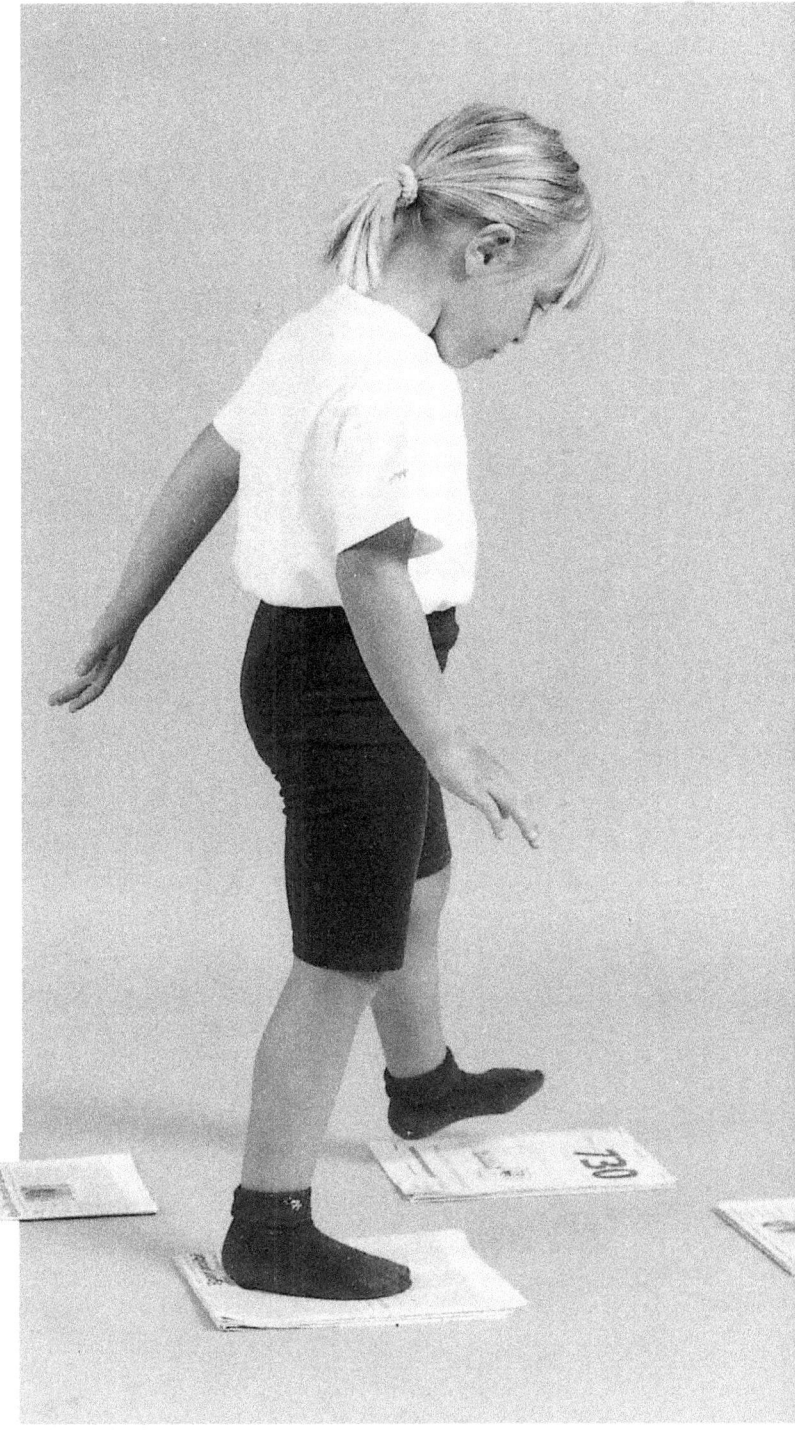

Exercise 5

The sheets of newspaper are placed one after the other, slightly apart to the right and to the left. The child hops from one sheet to the other without touching the newspaper, first with feet together and then with only one foot.

In this way, the child's capacity for a spatial organization is stimulated: the child has to know how to evaluate the length of the jumps he makes and the space occupied by his own feet between one jump and the next. In addition, they have to know how to dose the thrust, in order to maintain their balance.

Exercise 6

The child holds the newspaper in his hand, picks up a sheet of paper, puts it on the floor, stands on it with both feet and keeps his balance.
He then puts the second sheet of newspaper on the ground in front of him, stands on it and balances on one foot.

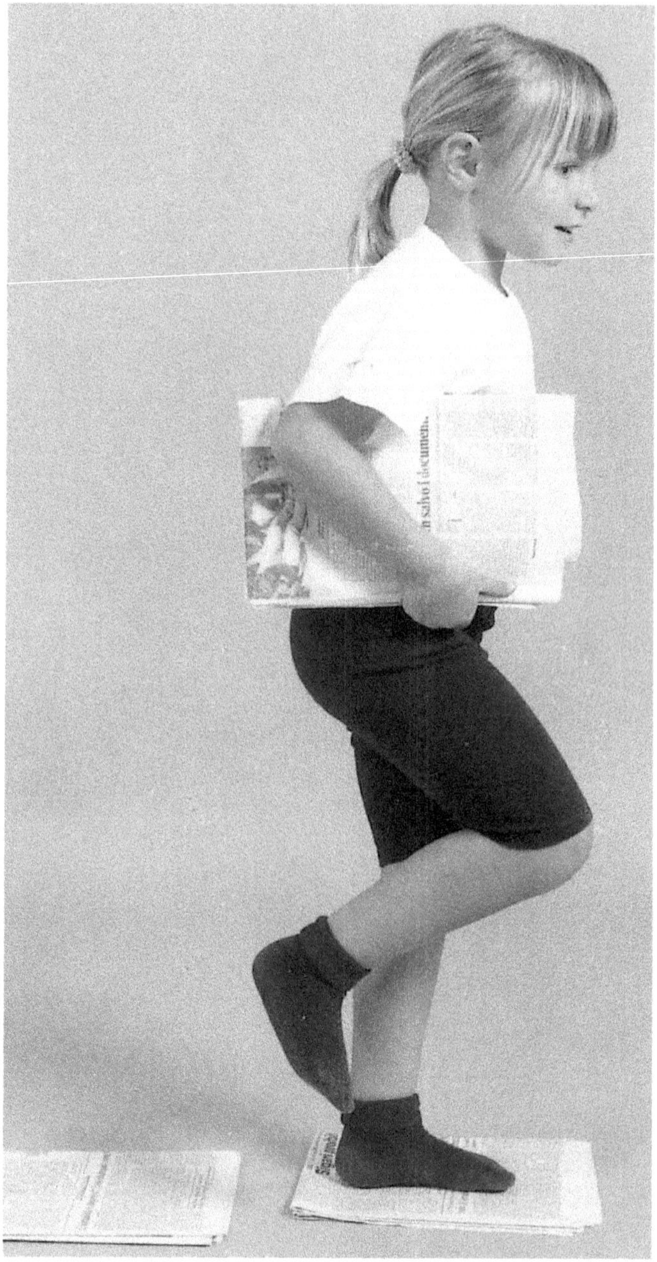

He returns again to the first sheet, on which he performs the first exercise, and to the second, on which he performs the second; he then places the third sheet on the floor, on which he sits, keeping his hands and feet off the floor and balancing on his buttocks.

The child can go back to the first sheet and repeat if he/she enjoys it, the sequence of exercises by inventing new ones up to the last sheet.

Through this progression, you are asked to make creative movements, stopping in one position: each leaf resting on the ground corresponds to a very precise movement that you will have to remember and carry out at the right moment.

GAMES WITH THE BALL

The ball is a must in a child's room, so it will be used in the series of games we propose here.

Since most of the exercises are done at home, a foam ball has been chosen to avoid possible damage and to make less noise.

The ball is an extremely important instrument from the point of view of motor development; thanks to it, the child learns to relate to an external object, coordinating his own movements with the movements and bouncing of the ball. In particular, the child learns to coordinate the action of the hands and feet with the visual information provided by the size and speed at which the ball spins and bounces.

In addition, countless group games can be invented with the ball the chapter in pairs and even alone.

Exercise 1

The ball is placed on the floor, the child stretches out on it with his belly on the ball, moves forwards and backwards naming the parts of the body that gradually come into contact with the ball.
This game is a simple way to help the child in the process of becoming physically and verbally aware of each part of his or her body.

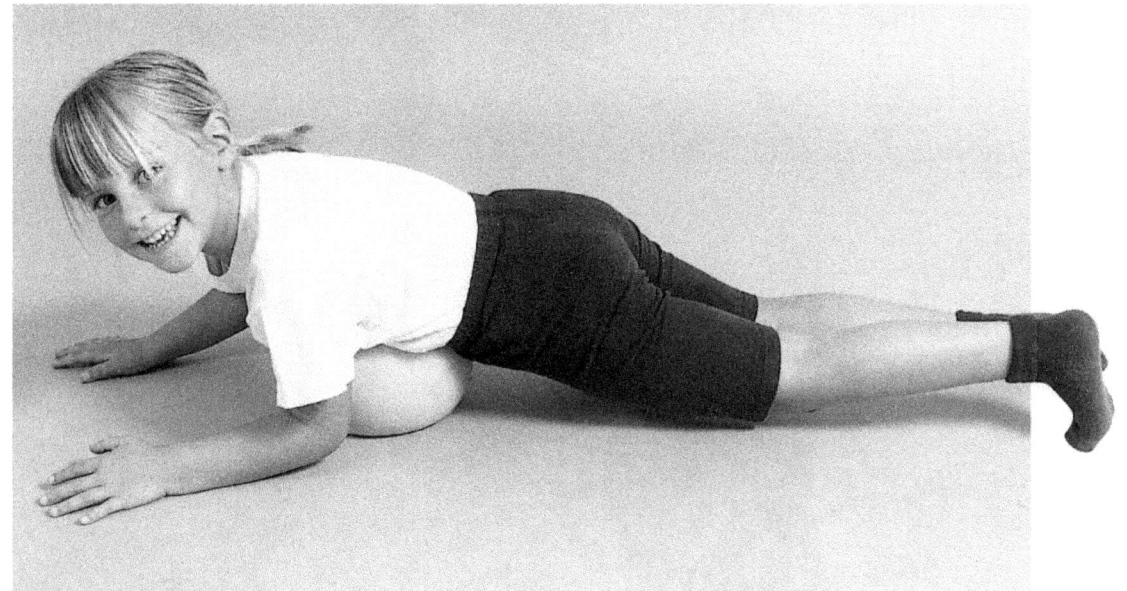

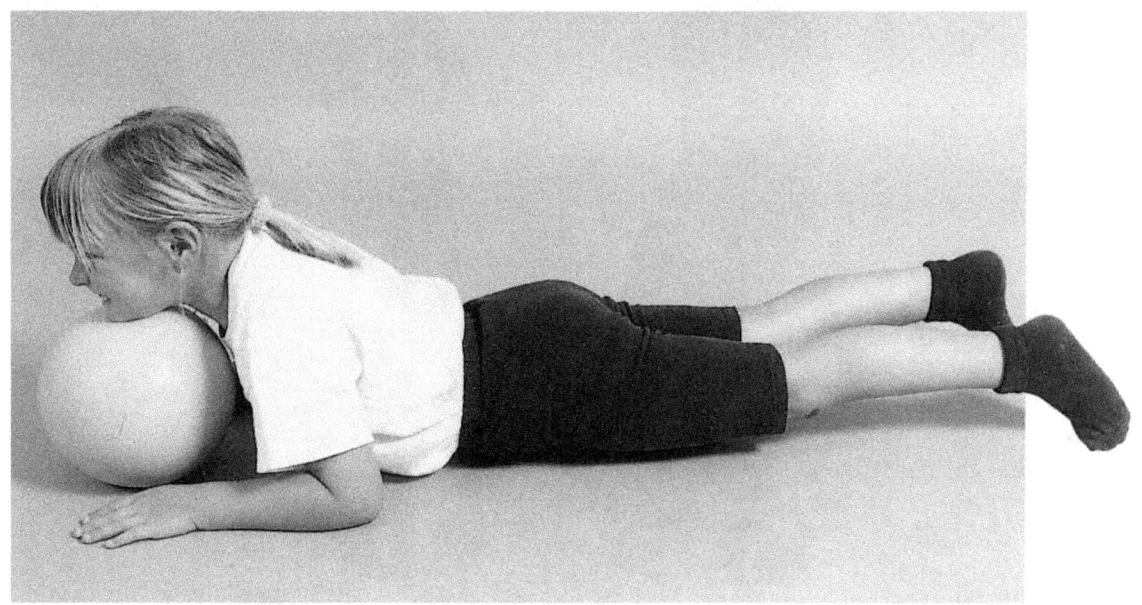

Exercise 2

Mother and child turn their backs to each other, standing upright; they pass the ball over their heads and then between their legs.

In this game, the child is asked to be able to judge the distance between his hands and the mother's and to make an appropriate movement, although in this case, visual information is not very helpful.

Exercise 3

The mother and child, face to face and a few metres apart, pass the ball to each other, spinning it on the ground.
This simple game allows the child to become familiar with the concepts of distance and speed by varying the intensity of the force to be applied to the ball.

Exercise 4

The child runs alongside the ball that the mother spins on the floor. This game requires the child to be able to match his speed to the speed of the ball and therefore helps him to develop spatial-temporal coordination.

Exercise 5

The child walks freely while the mother tries to hit him with the ball; if she succeeds, the roles are reversed.
This game requires the ability to aim and throw the ball and therefore develops inter-segmental coordination (throwing action) and spatial-temporal coordination (perception of the distance for the ball to cross).

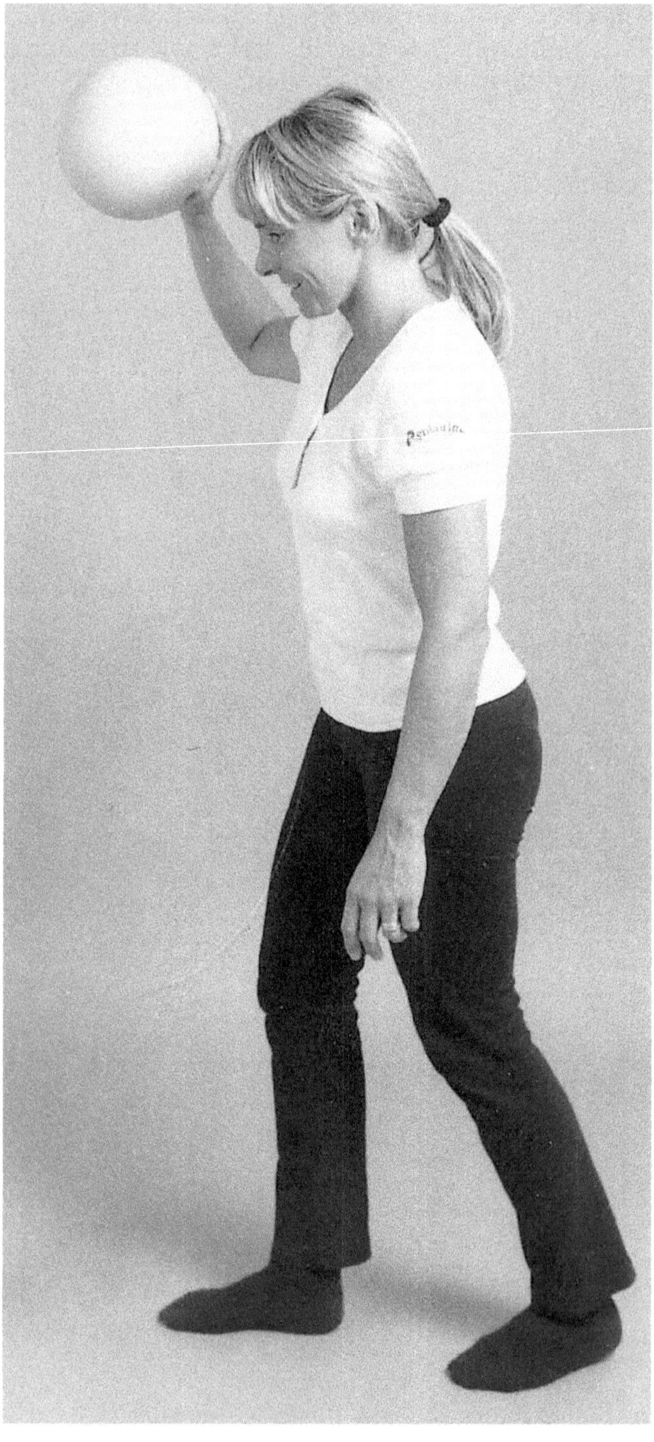

SEVEN TO TWELVE YEARS OLD

GAMES WITH THE BODY

The following games do not foresee the use of any instruments.
    They are generally games in pairs, intending to consolidate the capacity for strength, but also the development of fantasy, sociability, the ability to adopt a role and therefore to give free rein to the imagination and corporal expression. In addition to educating the sense of rhythm and its application to movement, it helps the child in the process of reinforcing the main motor schemes.

Exercise 1

The wheelbarrow

One child stretches out on the floor face down, leaning on outstretched arms while another holds him/her by the ankles. The child stretched out on the floor keeps his body rigid without swaying with his hips and walks on his hands, while the one standing holding him moves forward.

It is a strength game that mainly works the muscles of the upper limbs and trunk.

Exercise 2

The table

One child stands on all fours with his back on the floor (as seen in the previous exercises and in particular on page 48) and another holds his ankles and lifts them off the floor and then moves slowly forwards and backwards.
This is a strength game that works the muscles of the upper limbs and trunk (the so-called *body tone*).

Exercise 3

The sculptor

One child, who plays the role of the sculptor, positions the other, who plays the statue, in the desired way, moving his arms, legs, head, etc.; the statue has to maintain the position given to him. It is a game of imitation in which we put ourselves in the role of the sculptor and the statue; the statue has to show a great capacity for balance, while the sculptor can express all his fantasy.

Exercise 4

The mirror

One child stands in the desired shape, while the other child has to copy it as if it were the image of the mirror in which the first child is reflected.
It is a game of imitation in which they become aware of the different parts of the body and learn to recognize them on the other, also reinforcing the ability to distinguish right from left.

Exercise 5

The swing

Two children stand facing each other and hold hands: one bends the knees and then returns to an upright position while the other bends down. This is a simple coordination and tuning game that strengthens the muscles of the lower limbs.

Exercise 6

One child claps his hands and changes the rhythm while the other tries to put his foot on the ground at the same time.
This game helps the child to develop a sense of rhythm; in fact, he/she must be very attentive to the moment when the partner claps his/her hands and make the footrest coincide with the emission of the sound.

Exercise 7

Standing pulse

Two children stand facing each other and hold each other by the right hand, keeping the left foot close to each other. Pushing and stretching, each tries to knock the other off balance. The one who gets the other child's left foot off the ground first loses.

As the name of the game says, it is about *arm wrestling*, a presentation of strength but also of balance and cunning; in fact, the winner is not always the strongest, as in a classic arm-wrestling match, but the one who takes the opponent by surprise, pushing and pulling with the right intensity and at the most opportune moment.

Exercise 8

Pulse on the ground

This is the classic pulse that we are all familiar with, although children should stretch out on the floor because it is a more comfortable and natural position for them.
Two children lie on their stomachs and shake hands with their right hand on the ground and then arm wrestle. The winner is the one who is the first to place the back of the opponent's hand on the ground.
It is a performance of pure strength in which no other capacities are required, only the ability to resist the effort for as long as possible.

Exercise 9

One child stands on all fours, leaning on his hands and knees, while another tries to move him.
This is a strength game that works the muscles of the whole body of the person on the ground, especially the upper limbs, and the trunk of the person trying to move the partner.

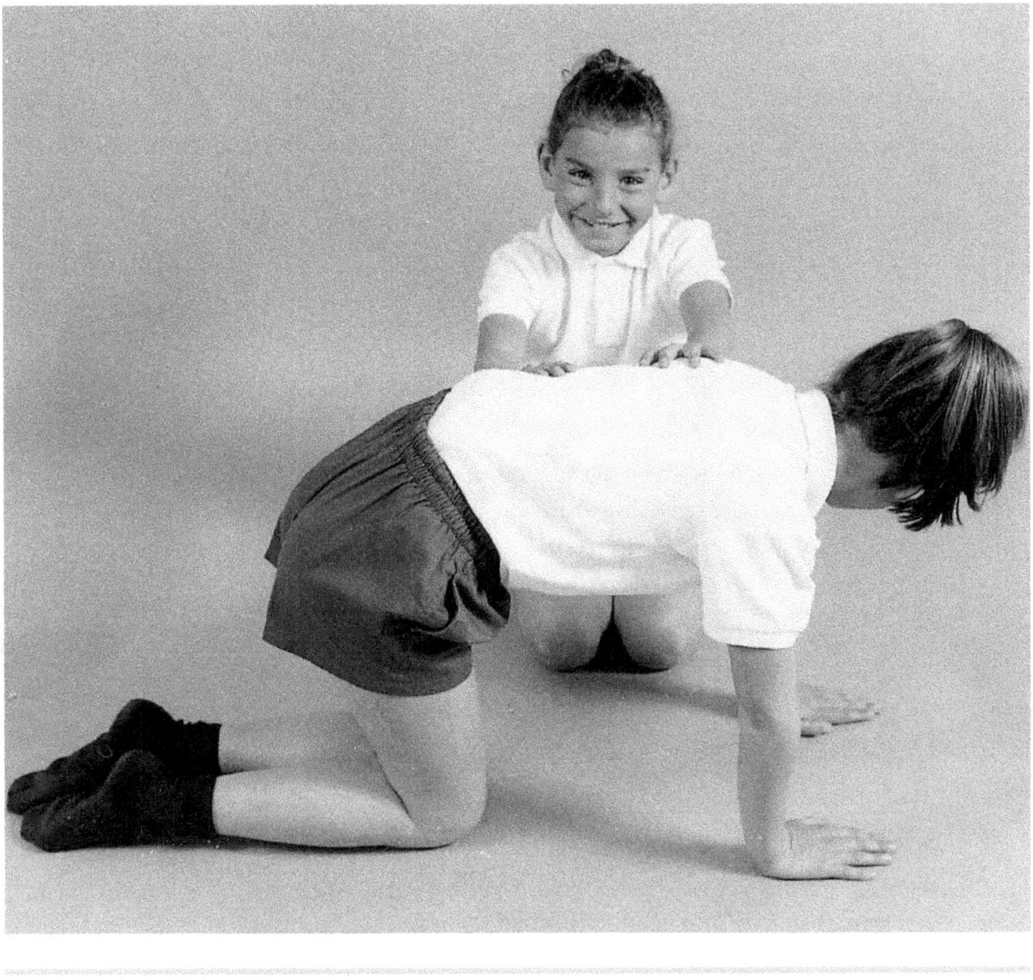

Exercise 10

One child stretches out on the floor face down and the other tries to turn him/her.
It is a game of strength that works all the muscles of the person who is stretched and the muscles of the upper limbs of the person who is trying to move the partner.

Exercise 11

One child lies face down on the floor while the other, standing on top of him, has to prevent him from getting up.
It is a game of strength that works a large part of the muscle groups of both children.

Exercise 12

One child crosses his arms in front of his chest, keeping the palms of his hands in contact with his shoulders: another child has to try to push his partner's hands away from his back.
This game develops the strength of the upper limbs.

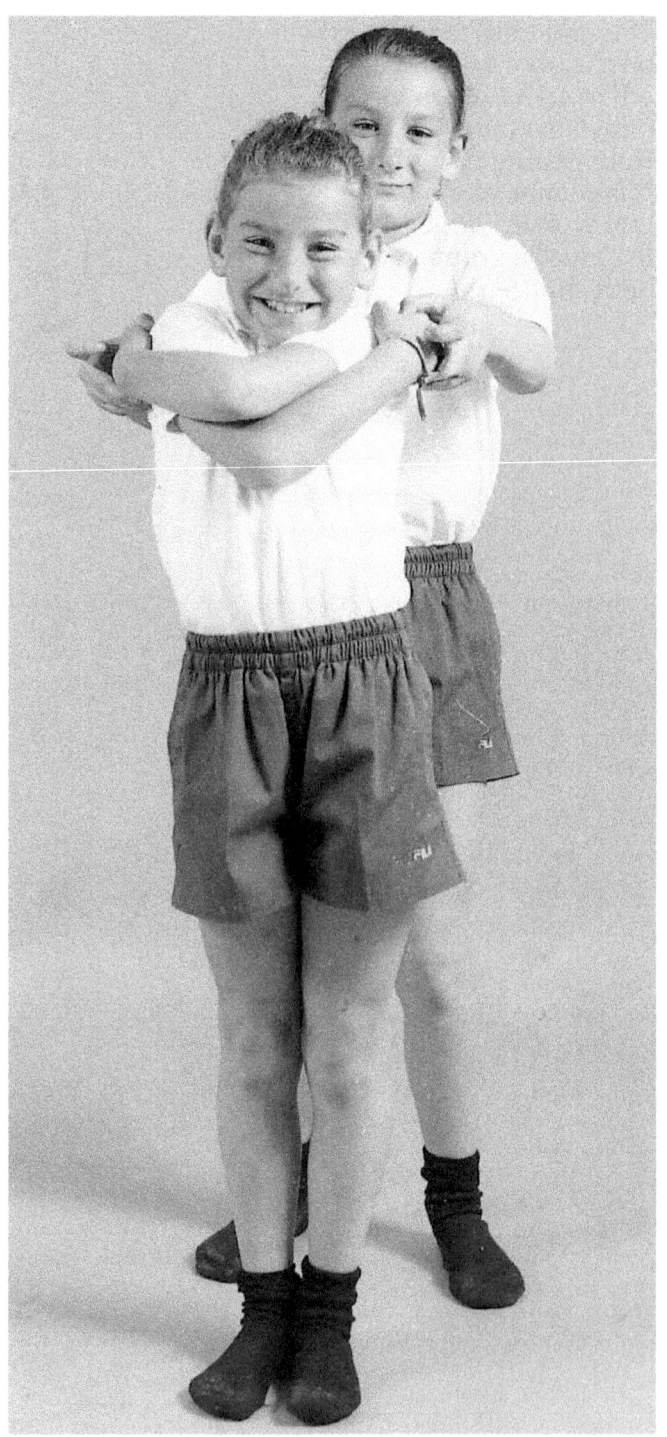

Exercise 13

The Balance

Two children stand facing each other, feet together, holding hands, and bend their knees at the same time while trying to keep their balance. This game develops the strength of the upper limbs and trunk and also requires good balancing skills.

Exercise 14

One child stands with his or her back to the other, who rests the palms of his or her hands on the back of the first and then pushes forward the partner, who puts up minimal resistance.
In this game, the strength of the pusher's upper and lower limbs is developed, as well as the muscles of the lower limbs and trunk of the resister.

Exercise 15

Two children, facing each other, hold hands and try to walk backwards pulling each other.
In this game, the general strength capacities applied to the motor scheme of throwing are developed.

Exercise 16

Two children, facing each other, palms together, push each other, trying to stop their opponent.
In this game, the general force capabilities applied to the thrust motor scheme are developed.

Exercise 17

A child holds another child with his back to him, around the waist: the trapped child tries to run forward.
In this game, the general strength capabilities applied to active and passive traction motor schemes are developed.

Exercise 18

Two children stretched out on their backs and with their legs squared try to move each other's legs by pushing them downwards.
In this game, strength is developed, in particular, the strength of the lower limbs.

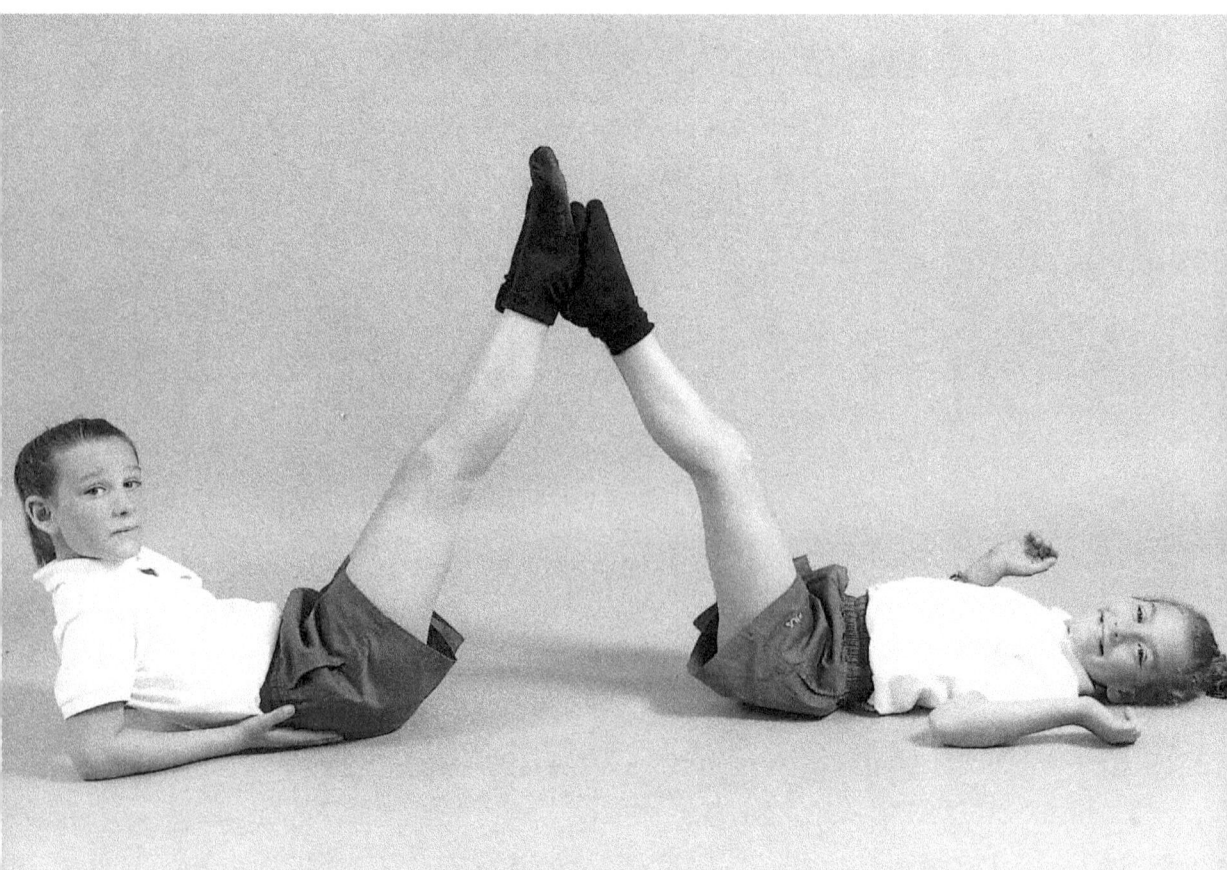

ROPE GAMES

Also with older children, the use of a rope makes it possible to invent situations and games that are particularly stimulating in terms of the ability to balance, both in a static and dynamic sense; moreover, these games play an important role in the process of consolidating spatial organization, as they help the child to perceive space in its various forms: above and below, in front and behind, right and left, etc.

Exercise 1

The rope is stretched out on the ground and a child walks on it.
When another child claps his hands, the one walking on the rope has to stop while keeping his balance.

The parry is performed on one foot only when a single clap is heard.

When he/she hears two claps, he/she should stand on two points of support, a hand and a foot, for example. The child walking on the rope will prepare to stop on a third support point when he/she hears three claps. And so on up to four or more if desired.

This game develops the ability to balance and stimulates the ability to relate a movement to an auditory sensation. On hearing the number of claps, the child must adopt certain positions and hold them on a small support surface.

Exercise 2

The rope is stretched out on the ground; two children, with their feet on it, are each at one end. They walk on the rope carefully so as not to fall. When they are close, they turn around and walk backwards. This exercise stimulates the ability to balance in a dynamic situation and on a restricted support surface: the rope. It, therefore, requires more attention than walking freely on the ground.

Exercise 3

The rope is stretched out on the floor. Two children, with their feet on it, each at one end, turn their backs to each other; they walk backwards until they meet and then return to the starting point.

The difficulty of this game lies in the fact that, when walking backwards, there is no possibility to see where the feet rest; therefore, this stimulates the children to be as attentive as possible to the tactile sensation that their own foot receives and that represents the only information thanks to which the next step on the rope can be made.

Exercise 4

The rope is stretched out on the ground and two children walk facing each other on the rope. When they meet, they swap places by holding hands and continue to the other end of the rope.
This game requires good balance and coordination skills and a good rapport between the two children.

Exercise 5

The rope is stretched out on the floor. Two children, facing each other, with their feet resting on it, shake hands and, by pulling, try to unbalance their opponent.

Whoever lifts one foot off the rope first loses.

As in the "Standing Pulse" exercise (see p. 86), this game, which requires a good deal of balance, also develops the ability to be strong, as well as the cunning to dose and perform the right stretches and thrusts at the right moment.

Exercise 6

The rope is tied to a support (table leg, chair, etc.) and one child holds the rope while another jumps over it.
Then, the child goes underneath by bending his knees.
Finally, he bends his back while balancing on both feet.
Through this game, the child learns to value space and, above all, the space occupied by his or her own body.
In the attempt to pass under an obstacle, represented in this case by the rope, he learns to distinguish the difference between above and below and relates this to the capacity for spatial organization.

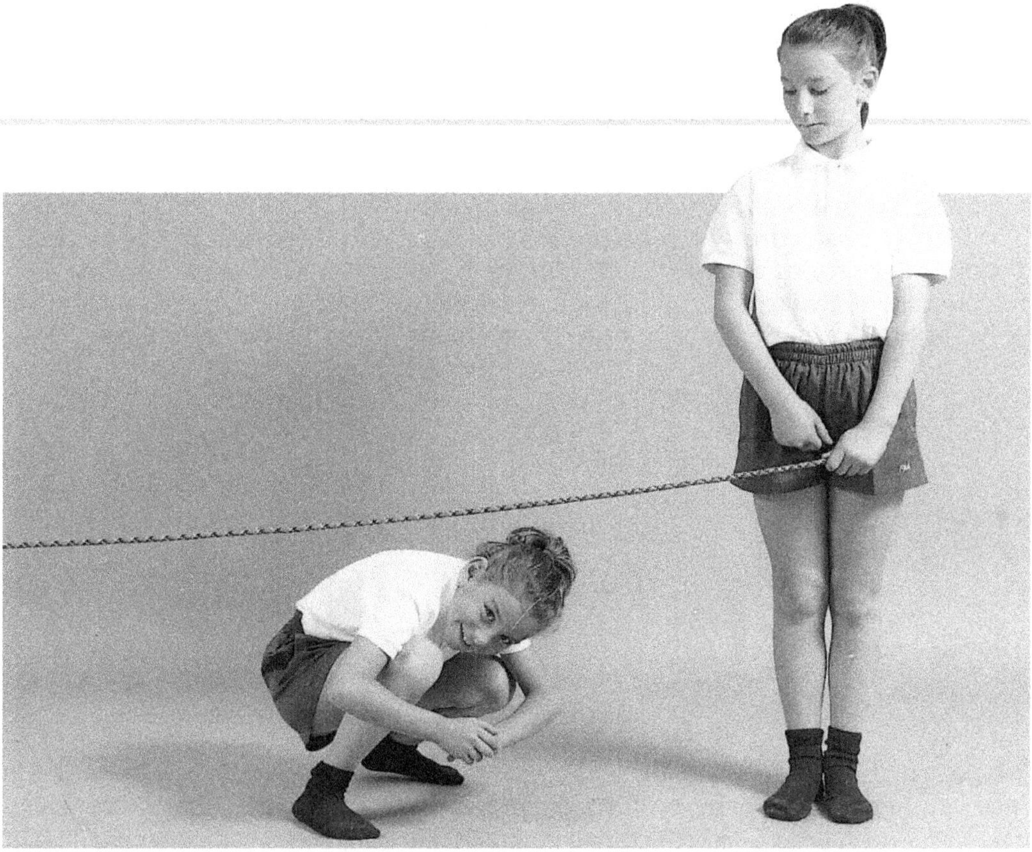

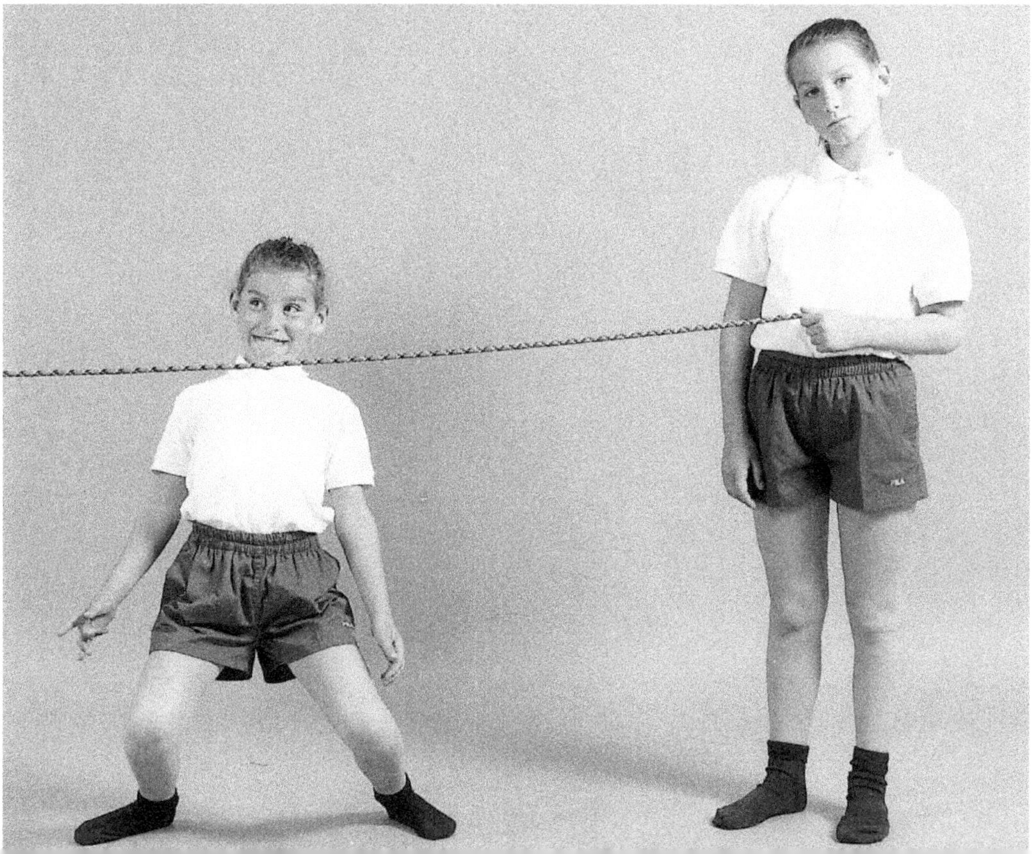

GAMES WITH THE BALL

The ball is one of the favourite toys at this age.

The exercises presented below are based on throwing and catching and help to consolidate coordination skills between sight and hands (oculo-manual), between sight and foot movement (oculo-podal) and between the space available and the rapid movement of the ball (spatiotemporal). By using the ball, it is also possible to create countless and varied game situations in which the child spontaneously feels stimulated to give his best to beat his opponent.

Exercise 1

While one child stands with his legs apart, the other will pass the ball under his legs, rolling it along the floor with his hand and then propelling it with his foot.

This game tests his spatial organization skills; before rolling the ball, they have to calculate the distance it has to cross and the size of the space through which it has to pass. In addition, the force to be applied to the ball has to be calculated.

Exercise 2

One child stands with his arms in front of him and his hands joined together, forming a hoop. Another child throws the ball, trying to get it between the arms of the first child. In this game, it is necessary to have a good capacity for spatial organization and spatial-temporal coordination, as well as certain throwing skills, as it is necessary to calculate the distance the ball has to cross and the position of the basket.

Exercise 3

A boy kicks the ball and runs alongside it, reaching for it and trying to stop it with one foot.
However, you can also let it pass between your splayed legs.
You can also reach it and stop it by sitting on it if you prefer.

This game requires a good capacity for spatial organization, a certain mastery of time perception and optimal spatial-temporal coordination. When rolling the ball, the child has to know how to dose the force to be applied, to run at a slightly higher speed than the ball to overtake it and to have enough time to turn and stop it with the foot, to pass it between the two feet or, finally, to stop it by sitting on it.

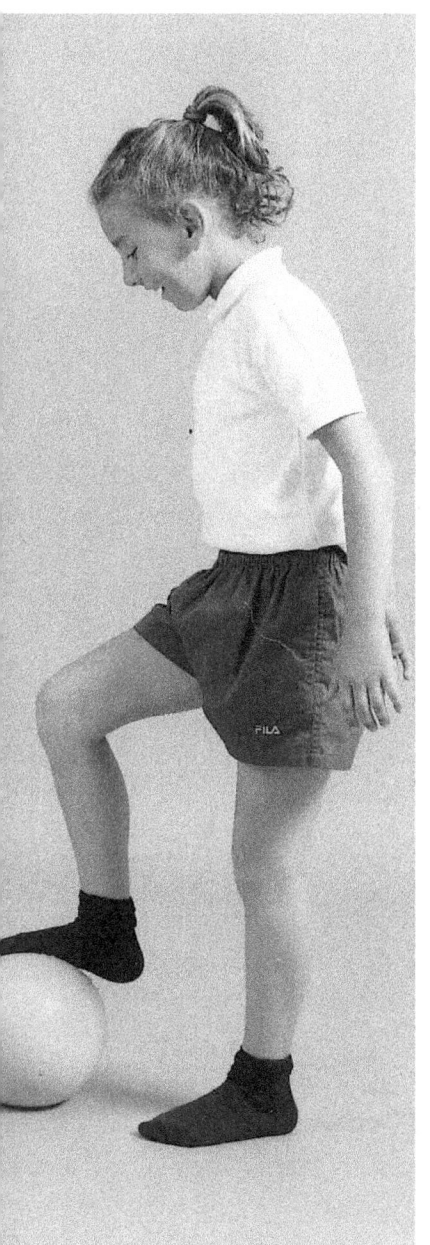
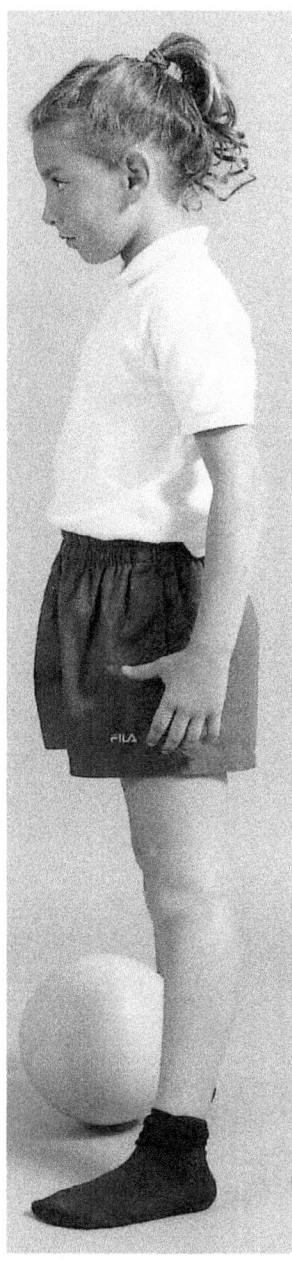
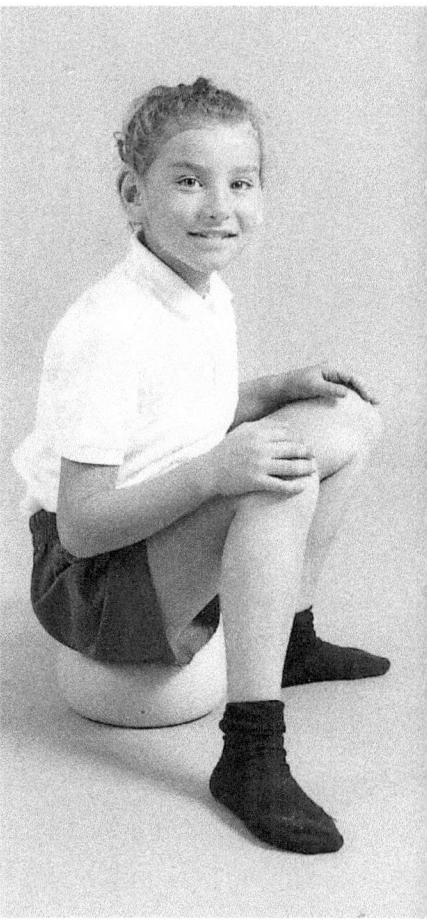

Exercise 4

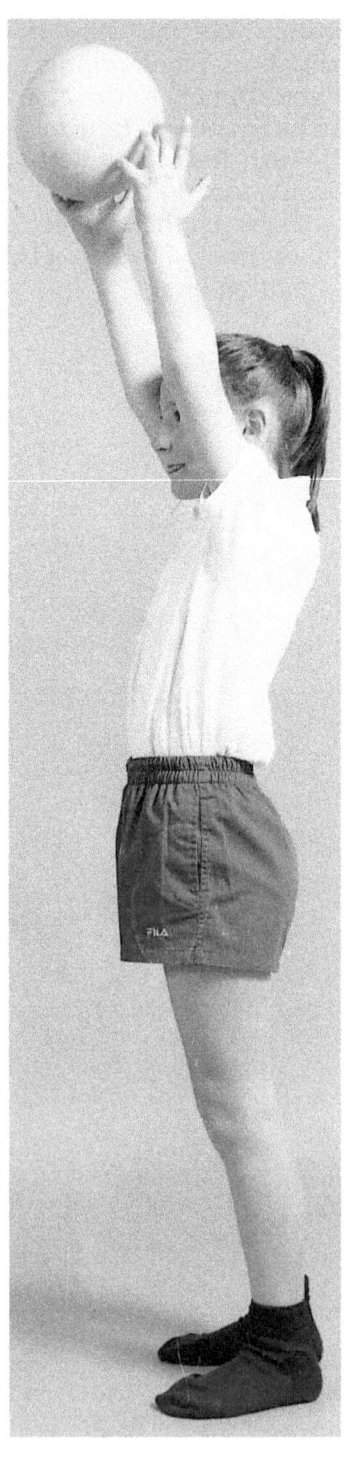

Two children stand facing each other: one passes the ball to the other, who receives it with both hands.

If you wish, you can also pick it up with one hand or even try to stop it on the ground with your foot.

As in all games in which the ball is thrown and received, these simple passes also require optimal initial coordination but, above all, spatial-temporal, oculo-manual and oculo-podal coordination. The first is essential to calculate the speed of the ball and the time it will need to cross a certain distance, while the second is fundamental to be able to catch or stop it at the right moment.

Catching with both hands is undoubtedly easier than catching with one, as in this case the impact of the ball must be cushioned so that the catch cannot escape.

The reception on the ground with the foot also presupposes the ability to anticipate the parabola made by the ball, together with a good sense of timing and optimal coordination of the movements of the foot.

Exercise 5

Two children, facing each other, make the passes with the ball, always in different ways.

From the chest

With both hands above the head

One-handed from the side

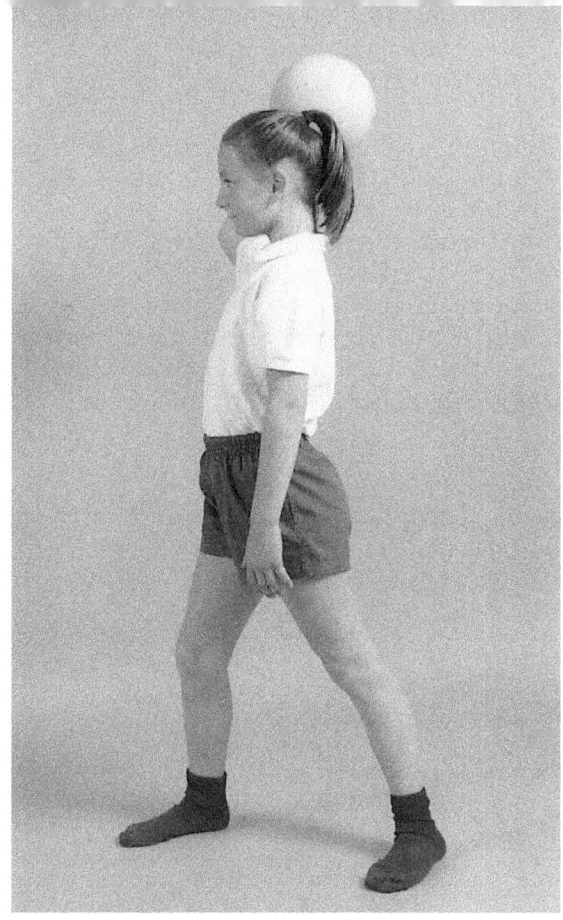

One-handed, as in baseball

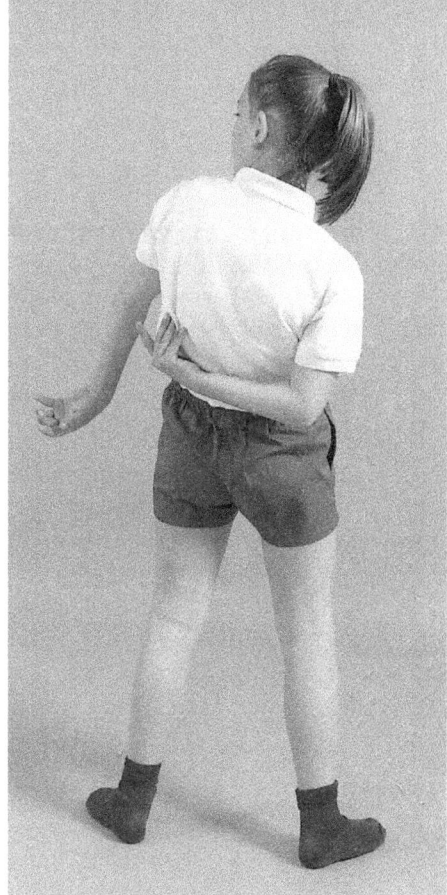

Behind the back

Below the legs

These passes aim to consolidate throwing and catching skills and require good basic coordination skills in addition to eye-hand and spatial-temporal coordination.

Exercise 6

Two children, facing each other, pass the ball to each other by performing a jump during the throwing phase and a hop during the catching phase.
This game presupposes complete mastery of the motor scheme of throwing and catching; it also requires, in addition to spatial-temporal and oculo-manual coordination, a good sense of timing that allows the throwing and catching action to be performed at the exact moment that coincides with the jump.

Exercise 7

One child bounces against the ground while another tries to steal the ball. When he succeeds, the situation is reversed and the game continues. This game presupposes the ability to bounce the ball. The fact of being in front of an opponent stimulates the child to strive for improvement and victory.

ROPE AND BALL GAMES

The simultaneous use of these two elements makes it possible to diversify the games considerably, providing increasingly complex and difficult situations and stimuli from a motor point of view, making them suitable even for older children.

The skills necessary for the use of the ball, such as spatial, spatial-temporal and oculo-manual coordination, are now brought into play together with the ability to balance (static and dynamic) which is required, on the other hand, when using the rope. In this way, situations are created in which the child is asked to perform an activity that requires greater motor development.

Exercise 1

The rope is stretched along its entire length on the floor. Two children, standing on it, pass the ball to each other, taking care not to put their feet outside.

This game presupposes complete mastery of the motor scheme of throwing and catching, which are performed while maintaining balance on a small surface.

Exercise 2

The rope is stretched out on the ground. Starting from the ends, two children pass the ball to each other while walking back and forth. Through this game, the child is asked to throw and catch the ball in a situation of unstable balance, as he/she is walking back and forth and, concentrating on the ball to be thrown, cannot see the surface on which he/she is resting his/her feet with each step.

Exercise 3

The rope is stretched out on the ground.
One child walks on it back and forth making ball passes to another child who moves freely around it.
Through this game, the child is asked to throw and catch the ball in a situation of unstable balance; he is concentrated on the ball and therefore cannot see the thin surface of the rope on which he has to rest his feet while his partner, away from the rope, can throw and catch the ball as he likes.

Exercise 4

The rope is stretched out on the ground, two children stand on their backs and pass the ball over their heads and then between their legs. Through this game, the child is asked to be able to assess the distance between his hands and those of his partner and to perform an appropriate movement even without visual information and in conditions of unstable balance.

GROUP GAMES

We have talked a lot about the need to play and to do gymnastics (or to do gymnastics while playing). It seems interesting to us, after having proposed exercises for one or two children, to present some games, with the same purpose, for larger groups. Some can be done at home, even in small rooms; others require larger spaces such as gymnasiums or gardens; some can be done without any equipment, while others require a ball, a rope or a simple handkerchief. Nevertheless, they are all suitable for children of any age, although they will be most appreciated by five or six-year-olds. To coordinate the games, the intervention of an animator is always necessary, who in this case can also be the mother, father, babysitter, etc.

All these exercises are preceded by a title that helps to identify the development and the objective more easily.

BODY-ONLY GAMES

These games are the easiest to organize and carry out, precisely because they do not require any tools. The children are always presented with new situations in which they are asked to solve problems of a motor nature, either in support of their peers (the team spirit begins to take shape in this way) or in opposition to them.

Some games concern the ability to pay attention and react to a stimulus ("Listen and go away", "The keyword", "The signal"); others call on the sense of rhythm, the ability to mentally represent movement ("Up and down") or spatial organization ("Change of house").

Exercise 1

Above and below

The children stand in front of the animator. When he shouts, "down!" the children squat down. When you shout, "up!" the children stretch their legs and stand up.
The animator can even trick them by making the opposite movement to the one indicated; the child who makes a mistake is eliminated. The winner is the one who manages to stay alone with the animator.

Exercise 2

Listen and go

Four or five children stand in single file. The animator claps his hands: with one clap the first in the line runs to the back; with two claps the last one runs to the head. The game continues and children who move at the wrong time or in the wrong direction are eliminated until only one child, the winner, is left.

Exercise 3

The train and the driver

The children stand in a single file, with their eyes closed and their hands on the shoulders of the partner in front; the last child, the engine driver, guides the "wagons" from behind by tapping on the shoulders of the last one who, in turn, will tap the "wagon" in front until he reaches the "locomotive" which will change its position according to the information received: a tap on the right shoulder means turn right; a tap on the left shoulder, turn left; a tap on both shoulders, stop; two taps on both shoulders, start walking.

Exercise 4

The thieves and the treasure

One child, blindfolded, sits on the floor with a handkerchief or a ball in front of him in the centre of the circle formed by the other children. In turn, as the animator points to a child, he or she approaches the treasure to steal it; if the child guardian notices this, he or she tries to touch the thief who, if caught, must take the guardian's place inside the circle. If the thief manages to steal the treasure, he returns to his place to continue the game with another thief.

Exercise 5

Change of house

The children are divided into groups of three; two hold hands to form the house and the third, in the middle, is the tenant. One child has to stand outside to ask for a change during which he/she will try to take a place as a house or as a tenant. If he shouts, "tenant change!" the houses stay in place while the tenants change places. Whoever stays out orders the next change. If he shouts, "change house!" the tenants stay in place while the houses are broken up and re-formed by new players around the tenants. On the command, "all change!" everyone has to find a new partner for the house, which will have a new tenant.

Exercise 6

The signal

The children are placed in several rows: each row forms a team behind a line. The first child in each line must run to reach the line on which the animator is standing when the animator gives the signal that he/she has previously declared. The animator can try to trick them by indicating the signal with a wrong movement.
If, for example, the cheerleader claps twice and the agreed signal was only once, the exit is not valid. If the signal is for the cheerleader to touch his nose, it is not valid if he touches his forehead.
Whoever moves at the wrong time causes the home team to lose a point; whoever reaches the finish line first wins.

Exercise 7

The keyword

The children are seated on the floor in a line. The keyword is chosen - e.g. *house* - and the animator explains a story: "Once upon a time there was a boy who lived with his parents and his five siblings in a small *house* near the river.' When the keyword is pronounced, the children have to run to the marked line: the last one to arrive is penalized.

Exercise 8

The network

The children stand in two lines, facing each other; the members of one line stand with their legs spread apart, with their feet touching their neighbour's feet, and hold hands with their arms raised and their eyes closed.
At the instructor's command, the children in the second line have to pass between the legs of their partners in the net without touching them. Whoever touches a child in the net is exchanged with him.

Exercise 9

The cage

Half of the children stand in a circle, holding hands with their eyes closed. The others stand inside the circle. On the animator's command, the children inside the cage try to get out without touching it. Whoever does so becomes a prisoner and can no longer get out. Then, the one who has freed himself enters again and the game is repeated until all the children are caged. Then the roles are reversed: those who were in the cage go into the circle and vice versa. The team that cages all its opponents in the shortest time wins.

Exercise 10

The garments

The children stand in a line, sitting on the floor behind a pre-established line.
The animator, at a certain distance, asks the children to close their eyes and takes off, for example, his jumper or a shoe, or folds his sleeves. He then asks the children to open their eyes and guess what has changed on him: the first one to know runs to the animator and, on reaching his side, gives him the answer. If it is accurate, he/she wins a certain score. The game is repeated until one of the children reaches the total number of points.

Exercise 11

The blind hen

The children are arranged in a circle, sitting on the floor. The facilitator chooses the child who is to play the role of the blind hen and blindfolds him/her. He/she has to go up to a partner and, by touching his/her face, guess who it is; if he/she guesses, the role is exchanged with him/her, and if he/she does not guess correctly, he/she tries another partner.

GAMES WITH THE BALL

Ball games require good hand-eye coordination and effective spatial-temporal perception: children are stimulated to develop these skills through ever-changing situations in which they must do their best to win.

In particular, children improve their catching action ("Air, Land, Sea") and throwing action ("Stop", "The Bears"), control of the movement and speed of the ball ("The Grasshopper") and learn to appreciate the strength, speed and rhythm applied to movement.

Exercise 1

The viper

The snake is represented by the ball, which must not be touched because it is dangerous. The children are seated on the floor in a circle, very close to each other. The animator starts the game by throwing the ball in the middle of the circle; the children try to push the ball away with their hands as soon as it reaches them. A child who is "bitten" by the ball on any other part of the body is "dead" and must turn on his back. The winner is the one who comes last without being bitten.
The same game can be played with more fun with a variant: half of the children are within the circle and the other half is available to form the circle outside from which an attempt will be made to hit children who are escaping to the centre to avoid being touched by the ball.

Exercise 2

Air, land, sea

The children stand in a semicircle in front of the animator, who holds the ball in his hand. The animator throws or rolls the ball on the ground towards a child who has to stop it with his feet if the animator has shouted, "sea!" with his knees if he has shouted, "earth!" and with his head if he has shouted, "air"!

Exercise 3

Stop

The children sit in a circle and the ball sits still in the centre on the floor. The animator calls the name of one child, who has to run and catch the ball; the others run and stop when the selected child catches the ball and shouts "stop". The ball must then be thrown at one of the stationary partners. The child who receives the ball stops. Then they get back in a circle and the game starts again.

Exercise 4

The grasshopper

The child who is to play the grasshopper sits in the centre of a circle formed by his or her peers; the grasshopper cannot rest because the peers try to hit his or her feet with a ball that they keep rolling on the ground. The player who manages to touch the grasshopper with the ball takes his place. The ball does not have to be thrown but must roll on the ground.

Exercise 5

The bears

The ball is placed on the ground in the centre of a large space; the children form two teams, the brown bears and the white bears, who line up facing each other, leaving the ball in the centre of the field.

Each team chooses a captain, the chief bear. When the animator shouts, "white bears!", the white bears will run into the field of the grizzly bears, who in turn will do the opposite. In the meantime, a grizzly bear, previously designated in secret by his captain, will pick up the ball and try to throw it at a white bear. The player hit will be excluded from the game; if the team captain is hit, the game is won. If not, the game shall be replayed alternately.

ROPE GAMES

The string is very useful for learning spatial organization, an important aspect of the exercises proposed here. It is an instrument that helps to define the field and therefore provides important information about space, distance, size and the concepts of above and below, in front and behind, right and left.

Exercise 1

Deer and leopards

The children stand in two lines, one of deer and one of leopards, facing each other. The rope is stretched on the ground between them. The animator shouts, "crows!" and the crows turn and run to the marked line. The one who is caught before reaching the line becomes a leopard. If the animator shouts, "leopards!" it is the leopards that escape.

Exercise 2

Mirrors and puppets

The children stand in two lines, one of puppets and one of mirrors, both facing each other. The string is on the floor between them. If the animator gives the command, "one step forward!" the puppets move forward and the mirrors move back. If the command is "two steps to the left!" the puppets will move to the left and the mirrors to the right.

The roles of the mirrors and puppets are then reversed and new movements are invented. The one who makes a mistake takes the place of the child in front of him or her and thus exchanges one role for another.

Exercise 3

In the sea, on the shore

The children stand around the rope placed on the floor so that it forms a circle. When the animator orders, "sea!" all the children jump into the circle; when he orders, "ring!" the children have to jump out until someone makes a mistake. The winner is the last one without making a mistake.

SEA!

GLOSSARY

On all fours: leaning on hands and knees.

Support: part of the body in direct contact with the ground.

Shrunken: legs bent, trunk and head bent.

Indian row: the children are positioned one behind the other with their foreheads facing the same direction.

Line: the children stand side by side with their foreheads facing the same direction.

Legs bent: with knees bent.

Legs apart: with feet apart.

Feet parallel: with one foot beside the other.

Prone: face down.

Supine: face up.

Trunk bent: with the head close to the legs.

Vertical: resting on hands with arms, trunk and legs straight.

Somersault: rotation of the body about its own longitudinal axis.

www.ingramcontent.com/pod-product-compliance
Lightning Source LLC
Chambersburg PA
CBHW080604170426
43196CB00017B/2896